100 WAYS TO GET YOUR CHURCH NOTICED

Other books by Neil Pugmire

Published by Kingsway:
50 Seasonal Sketches

Published by the Bible Reading Fellowship:
The Adventures of the J Team (with Sue Hodge)
Launchpad (with Mark Rodel)

100 Ways to Get Your Church Noticed

NEIL PUGMIRE

KINGSWAY PUBLICATIONS
EASTBOURNE

First published 2006

Illustrations by Nigel Rouse
Design for cover by CCD (www.ccdgroup.co-uk)
ISBN-10: 1842912402
ISBN-13: 978-1-842912-40-9

KINGSWAY COMMUNICATIONS
Lottbridge Drove, Eastbourne BN23 6NT, England.
Email: books@kingsway.co.uk
Printed in the USA

Contents

CONTENTS

CONTENTS

CONTENTS

Foreword

At the end of Matthew's Gospel, Jesus commissioned his
disciples to preach the gospel to the whole world. In other
words, communication is central to mission. The past few
decades have seen an explosion of new forms of communications technology. Mobile phones, e-mail and the internet
have revolutionised the way we interact with each other,
and have intensified our sense of global interconnection.

But they also mean that we are literally bombarded with
information. Somehow the Church must make its distinc-
tive voice heard amidst all the undifferentiated clamour.
And, of course, communication is not just verbal: it is also
through signs and actions. The Church must be visible if it
is to be noticed.

Neil Pugmire is an expert communicator. He is a journal-
ist, playwright, webmaster and publicist, with a passion for
generating public awareness about the Church and issues of
social justice. I believe his book is essential reading for all
who share the disciples' commission to proclaim the good
news of Jesus Christ in word and action.

In writing this book, Neil has done us a great service –
and probably saved us a great deal of time and effort. This is

not just a book to read: it is a tool to be used. I cannot think of any good reason not to get hold of a copy.

The Rt Revd Kenneth Stevenson
Anglican Bishop of Portsmouth

Introduction

In today's society, we can rarely do anything without something screaming for our attention, whether it's in-yer-face TV advertising, incessant text message updates, billboards plastered with designer logos or addictive web-based chat rooms. In a typical day, we will be exposed to more than 3,000 adverts – from the obvious ones in newspapers and on websites to more subtle commercial logos on supermarket plastic bags or the side of beer glasses.

Not surprisingly, many churches struggle to make their voices heard above the cacophony. Some still rely on methods they used 30 years ago to try to communicate their messages – the hand-drawn poster stuck to the church noticeboard, the photocopied parish magazine, or the verbal notice at the start of worship. Because there is so much more information for everyone to absorb these days, even regular churchgoers may miss the casual reference to an event or an opportunity.

Not only are some of the methods we use liable to be swamped by a thousand and one other things, but they may also be the wrong types of communication for the kind of people we want to attract. One survey has suggested that only around 15 per cent of the UK population are 'readers' – people who are comfortable digesting slabs of text in books, newspapers or committee minutes. Another 15 per cent of people are 'non-readers' – those who feel very uncomfortable reading anything. The vast majority, 70 per cent, are categorised as 'browsers'. Such people flick through newspapers and magazines, stopping to read only when an eye-catching headline or photo catches their attention. They are happy to read, but will quickly get bored.

Broadly speaking, the kind of people who go to church are likely to be older, wealthier and better educated than the majority of the population. Congregations and church leaders will tend to be among the 'readers' within the population. The type of communication they use tends to be text-based, rather than visual. Yet for the vast majority of people, this often isn't an attractive method of communication.

We live in a highly visual age, with umpteen digital TV channels to choose from, millions of snazzy, image-based web pages to look at, and well-designed glossy magazines in every newsagent. Give a 'browser' a typical piece of church literature, and it's unlikely to grab their attention for long.

So how can we make sure our churches, activities, events and people get noticed in this busy, secular, visual world? The ideas in this book incorporate those you might understand as 'publicity' in the normal sense – websites, posters, parish magazines, media liaison – and other ideas that have more to do with involvement with the local community or the look and feel of our church building. These also have a valuable role to play in our church's communications strategy. Word-of-mouth reputation is still important, even in a society where we rarely talk to our immediate neighbours. Think of how easy it is for a local school, hospital or garage to gain a good or a bad reputation, simply by friends chatting to each other. The same can, and does, happen to churches. Personal recommendations are also trusted more than glossy brochures.

The aim of communicating with the wider community is not *just* to 'get your church noticed'. The purpose behind this activity is to draw people closer to God. To encourage non-churchgoers to sample your activities, learn more of the gospel and develop their own faith, you may need to market your church as a vibrant, exciting community. But if you discover that your posters, leaflets and parish magazine articles are starting to glorify your church or its leaders rather than drawing people into a deeper spiritual life, you may be heading down the wrong track. One of the problems with imitating secular culture is that we can fall into the same traps of worshipping 'celebrity' rather than God himself.

Internal and external communication

Church communication includes two elements. Internal communication involves helping church members understand about the church's vision and priorities, teaching them about faith, and making sure they are aware about forthcoming events. It also involves making sure members can communicate with each other and provide feedback to the leadership. Communication is not just one-way: in the best churches, church members know that their leadership is listening and responding.

External communication involves communicating to those in the wider community about forthcoming events, how the church can help in times of need, worship services and the gospel message itself. This is, naturally, closely allied with mission and community engagement. It can involve trying to subvert misconceptions that people have about church in general, or your church in particular. It can involve appropriating some of the methods used by the secular world, such as branding, training in offering a welcome, and media liaison. Equally, it can be completely counter-cultural – offering to do menial, practical tasks for people you don't know is virtually unheard of outside Christian circles.

You may wonder why internal communication with those who already go to church is included in a book about getting your church noticed. Surely those who already come to your church know all about it? To a certain extent, they do (although there are probably some church activities they know nothing about). But the best adverts for church are actually the people who go regularly. If they know about your events well in advance, and your activities in some detail, their word-of-mouth recommendation will be well informed and passionate. If they don't, any invitation to non-churchgoers may be more vague or even non-existent.

Basic principles

The fact that we are still reading and absorbing Jesus' words and values 2,000 years after his earthly life suggests that he was an excellent communicator. He didn't have his own website, colourful posters or a book deal. But he displayed some important principles about communication that we would do well to study:

(i) He knew his message.

We often talk today about having some kind of 'mission statement' – a guiding principle behind all that we do. Jesus certainly knew what he was on earth for and what messages he wanted to emphasise over and over again, both in words and actions. He wanted people to repent, to be healed and to be set free; he wanted them to understand the good news about the new kingdom; he wanted to be inclusive to those on the margins of society. Theologically, some of these concepts might have been quite complex, but he expressed them simply and directly, repeated them often, and used actions as often as using words. Do we do the same?

(ii) He knew his audience.

Look at the kind of people Jesus was speaking to: first-century fishermen, farmers, tax-collectors and religious zealots. He knew their backgrounds, and what would appeal to them. That's why his parables were all about growing wheat, managing vineyards and caring for farm animals. And he also spoke in different ways to different people. He told the crowds entertaining parables, but explained the meaning behind them only to his disciples. He argued about religious hypocrisy with the Pharisees, but spoke in a quite different way to the woman caught in adultery. Do we also tailor our message to different audiences, or do we use the same methods each time?

(iii) He used stories and images.

Jesus' stories were easy to understand, even though he was conveying quite complex spiritual points about social justice, the afterlife or atonement. He rarely answered an abstract question with an abstract answer. He constantly used metaphors, visual aids and symbolic images. Some of his Sabbath healings are dramatic, visual examples of the nature of his new kingdom. He spoke about the 'living water' to the woman at the well, compared God's love to the devotion of a father for his wayward son, and used images of broken bread and outpoured wine to describe his own death. Jesus knew these images would be more memorable than any theological explanation. The ubiquity of the phrases 'Good Samaritan' or 'Prodigal Son', even in secular society, and the continuing use of Communion to remember Christ's death show that he was right. How often do we use symbols, metaphors, images and stories to convey our own faith?

These principles can inform our church communication in many ways. Knowing what our central message is helps us to create logos or identities that ram it home, to know exactly what to put on the home page of our website, and what to emphasise in our magazines. Knowing more about our 'audience' – the people who live in our locality, for the most part – helps us to tailor the methods we use more precisely for them. We may choose to use different methods to reach the council estate and the stately home. Equally, different methods will be appropriate for those with faith and those without, for the OAP and the teenager, and for the 'reader' and the 'browser'.

As churches seem to be less effective at communicating with the 'browser' or the 'non-reader', it's important to focus on some principles that might help us in this area. Here are three principles that could improve the quality of our communication to such people, based on the principles enshrined in Jesus' ministry:

(i) *Greater use of symbolism.*

The Church, historically, has been quite good at using symbols. Apart from the drama of a Communion service, there is the fish symbol we put on our cars to denote our faith, and the most recognised symbol throughout history: the cross, which has been used in church art, architecture and literature for 2,000 years to remind people of Jesus' death.

But, strangely, in a world full of competing logos and easy-to-read pamphlets, our church publications often remain stubbornly symbol-free. What about colour-coding the pages of our orders of service or our church website to make it easier for people to find their way around? Or what about an instantly recognisable logo to denote our particular church family that can be used on all our church's publications?

(ii) *Greater use of images and photos.*

Historically, the Church has quite a good record in this department too: witness the number of icons, statues or stained-glass windows designed to help us worship. The best examples of Christian literature will often use

images of young, smiling Christians enjoying themselves. Consciously, or sub-consciously, we take in a
message that joining in will make us happy.

Yet look at a typical parish magazine, church noticeboard, or even – incredibly – some church websites and
you may not find a single photo. There may be reports
of interesting events or even interviews with members
of the congregation, but no images to suggest what the
event or the person looks like.

The ease with which video images can be recorded
on camcorders or digital cameras and accessed via a
website, beamed onto large screens using a projector or
edited into a professional video or DVD, suggests that
the Church may be missing another opportunity. Moving images of people enjoying themselves at church
events may be even more persuasive than stills.

(iii) Greater use of stories.

Again, there is a good Christian heritage here – from
Jesus' parables, through medieval mystery plays to
modern-day Christian novels and sketches, stories
have always helped people understand faith better.
Preachers will know that the minute they stop talking
in the abstract and start an anecdote, people start to listen more intently. And there are many testimonies or
stories about people's experiences of faith within our
congregations that we could use.

But look at a typical church magazine, or piece of
outreach literature, and you may not find a single such
story. Imagine the difference it might make to your
church's leaflet about a basics course if there was a

photo of a real person and quotes explaining how much the course had helped them? Or what about using testimonies from congregation members in your magazine or on your website?

This is not to suggest we 'dumb down' church literature to appeal to a less literate populace, or even to ape secular publications that seem to be all design and no content. It's just that – in a world where people are often less familiar with church liturgy, church jargon and what Christians actually believe – anything that makes it easier for them to access our services or our publications has to be good.

How to use this book

In this book, you'll find practical suggestions designed to help Christians get their message across, using some of these principles. They don't come with a foolproof guarantee of success, but these tips should help willing congregations make more of an impact on the society they live in.

There should be food for thought for large and small congregations, from churches that only meet for Sunday worship to ones with active ministries taking place daily. Each of the 100 ideas is expanded on with a 'How To. . .' section and there are suggestions for where to find further resources.

In some sections, it's difficult to show exactly what is being suggested without reference to photos showing sample locations or designs. Because of the difficulty in reproducing photos in this kind of book, a companion website – www.getyourchurchnoticed.com – has been created for this purpose. You'll also find helpful downloads there, and there's also a chance for you to send in ideas of what your church is doing to help it get noticed.

The book assumes that you have some kind of influence to change the way things might be done in your church – perhaps you are a pastor, a vicar or a minister, or perhaps you serve as an elder, a PCC member or are in a leadership role of another kind. But don't worry if you aren't. You can still use this book to make suggestions to those who are in leadership.

Strategy

1. Set up a communications team to decide strategy and forthcoming priorities.

How do you decide how to communicate within your church or to the wider world? Is it always the same method – a few hastily chosen words to the congregation before a Sunday service? Or a handful of typewritten posters on your church noticeboard?

Does it depend on the event or the people involved? If your midweek over-60s group held a coffee morning for those who were recently bereaved, would they be left to think of how to publicise it themselves? Would they think of asking the webmaster to mention the event on the church website or writing a press release?

Then there's the question of strategy. Even if your church has agreed on an overall vision, you may discover little of that vision reflected in aspects of church communication. Perhaps what appears in the parish magazine or notice-board depends on who within your congregation has been most proactive in contributing. Despite your express focus on radical Christian discipleship, your website's home page may still be promoting a fundraising flower festival. And there may be little 'joined-up thinking' – your evangelism team may not have twigged that the flower festival, when hundreds of people come into the building, would be a good time to promote next month's evangelistic service.

Finally, there's the question of priorities. This is a tricky one, as churches generally like to encourage people who have ideas to go ahead and do things. Imagine that some congregation members want to perform a pantomime. There's nothing wrong with that – it's entertaining, it allows people to get to know each other better, and it may even raise funds. But it's all that people have been talking about for weeks. The noticeboard is plastered with posters for it and it dominates the verbal notices on the Sunday before the performance. Inevitably, the pantomime plays to a sell-out crowd.

But what happens to that special day when you hope to brainstorm your way towards a new vision for the church community? It's been mentioned in the weekly leaflet and parish magazine. But when the time comes, only a handful of diehards turn up because it didn't get as high a profile as the pantomime. Yet, arguably, it was a more important event. How can you ensure that such events don't get lost in the welter of other activities?

One way to do it is to create a team with specific respon-sibility for communications or publicity. They should act as the first port of call for any group hoping to publicise what they do, or hoping to put on an event. They should know how to communicate to those within your congregation as well as to the wider community. They should think stra-tegically about how the church calendar fits together – if necessary, giving advice to others about the best time of year to hold an event. They should also know your priorities – if this year's big push is about the church's commitment to children and young people, perhaps the publicity for the family-friendly Nativity play needs to take precedence over the carol service in the sheltered housing complex.

Of course, this team shouldn't just be a talking shop. Ideally, it should consist of those who actually *do* the communication in your church, as well as the leaders who can take strategic decisions about what happens when.

If yours is a smaller church where few people have the skills or resources to do these kinds of jobs, it might be worth checking to see whether you can form a communications team jointly with churches of other denominations in your area.

How to do it:

1. Get together those who are doing the communications jobs within your church at the moment (parish magazine editor, webmaster, weekly leaflet compiler etc.) and those within the church leadership who can take strategic decisions.
2. Organise meetings. They may need to happen monthly at first, but ultimately may only need to happen quarterly.
3. Furnish the communications team with the church's long-term vision or strategic priorities as decided by your church leadership. This may help determine the focus for publicity for the next six to twelve months.
4. Look at the existing church calendar. Decide which

events should be promoted most heavily, and which events can act as 'feeder' events to others – for instance, a church fete could be used to distribute publicity about a forthcoming special service.

5. Look at the activities that already happen in church. Which might you want to publicise most? It might be better to publicise activities that are thriving. Publicising a poorly attended group won't have the same impact!

6. Use that information to decide priorities for the next few months. Those in the team should use those priorities to determine what to feature on the front page of the parish magazine, the home page of the website, how many posters to print, and what to emphasise verbally in services.

7. Don't be afraid to keep hammering home a single message, if that happens to be your church's priority. Like an advertising slogan, the idea that St Martin's Church is 'open 24/7 for visitors' will eventually catch on within your congregation and community.

8. Discuss the possibility of a separate budget for church communications, or ensure that a publicity section is added to the budget for any major church event or activity.

9. Learn to say 'no' or 'maybe' to people's ideas. If your church calendar is already crammed with important events, don't try and squeeze another one in. Learn to suggest graciously that the idea is a good one, and that it might be more appropriate at a later date.

10. You may find yourself assailed with information about events at nearby churches, ecumenical projects,

diocesan events or national priorities. Choose carefully which of these you would like to support, perhaps prioritising those that fit in with your own church's plans.

2. Ensure a publicity element is taken into account in planning all church events and activities.

Whether you create a communications team or not, it helps to make sure that people are aware of the importance of publicity in planning events and activities within your church. This will usually involve some guidance by the church leaders to the organisers – checking that they have consulted with the communications team, or (if there is no team) that they have sufficient expertise to organise publicity themselves.

The publicity will usually involve letting both church members and non-churchgoers know about what's planned. This may take time and patience, but an eagerly anticipated event is better than one that arrives before it has registered in people's minds. Your congregation probably needs to be told about the event or activity half a dozen times in different ways before it actually reaches their diaries. It's therefore important to make sure that there is adequate time for the communications team (or the organisers themselves) to swing into action.

How to do it:

1. If you have a communications team, make sure they are given a high enough profile, so those organising events

or activities know to talk to them before planning anything.

2. Any requests for publicity should be referred to the communications team, who will need to think about how it
   fits into their current strategy, their priorities and the
   church calendar.

3. If necessary, a member of the communications team
   may need to attend a planning meeting to explain about
   publicity strategy, perhaps even encouraging the group
   to delay their plans to make sure enough publicity has
   been done beforehand.

4. If there is no such team, a church leader may need to
   check that the organisers have planned both a variety of
   methods of publicity and enough time for the message
   to seep through to both church members and non-
   churchgoers.

5. If an event or activity is a priority, ask your team to think
   of up to six different ways of publicising it, and make
   sure they do so.

**3. Think about the types of communication your
church may need to *stop* doing to release people's
time and energy in other areas.**

This is a hard one, as it is always difficult to say 'no' to
enthusiastic people within the congregation! But in a
church community, people are often busily doing things
because they have always been done in that way, rather
than thinking about how necessary they actually are. That's
especially true of church communications.

Imagine the typical monthly parish magazine. It takes an

editor two weeks each month to collect the articles, design the pages and get them photocopied on the church's antiquated machine. One team collates and staples pages together, and another delivers a hundred or so copies to people around the neighbourhood who are housebound or had a previous connection with the church. The rest are placed at the back of church for congregation members to pick up.

That's an enormous amount of effort in order to achieve . . . what? The vicar's letter is read by a few people, and some details of church events are circulated. But it only reaches the congregation members who bother to pick it up and a handful of people outside church. It has little impact on the local community. Yet because there has always been a parish magazine, it continues in the same vein.

Imagine the difference if the same amount of effort went into producing a professionally printed, full-colour news-letter, including photographs, that was only produced once or twice a year, but was posted through the letterboxes of every household in the local community as a form of out-reach. Some might feel intimidated at the time, energy and financial commitment that might involve. In fact, it might only be possible for them to do this if they *stopped* producing the parish magazine as they do at the moment.

How to do it:

1. Assess the various forms of communication used within your church. Be honest about the effectiveness of each method in getting the message across.
2. Think about what you may need to stop doing to release

the time, energy and money to consider some new ideas.

3. Think about the consequences of doing so: it may be, for instance, that former churchgoers who are now house-bound appreciate seeing a parish magazine each month. Perhaps a weekly pew sheet can be posted to them each week to keep them in touch? Perhaps they might appreciate the occasional pastoral visit?

4. Carefully explain the reasons why you want to stop doing something. Many of us dislike change. It's important that people understand that it's to make communication more effective.

5. If you can't create an overlap from the 'old' to the 'new' forms of communication, at least make sure the change happens seamlessly. People should notice that the change makes a real difference.

4. Make sure your communications strategy is regularly re-assessed to take account of changing situations.

A communications strategy that is appropriate now may not be relevant for ever. Not only are methods of communication changing quickly, but your church's priorities will change too. Your communications team may learn new skills and so can suggest new ways of doing things. And the membership of the group may change too, opening up new possibilities.

So it's important to build into your communications strategy the chance to re-assess it at regular intervals, perhaps annually. Of course, if your church itself regularly re-assesses its vision, it would be appropriate to tie it into that timescale. Imagine if your church's vision switched from concentrating on families with children one year to a focus on tackling world poverty the next – and the church displays changed within weeks to illustrate that changed priority.

How to do it:

1. Make sure you plan regular re-assessments of your communications strategy into the timetable of meetings of the communications team, ideally to coincide with alterations in the church's overall vision.
2. Try to ensure that members of your communications team can widen their expertise. Send them on courses, buy them the necessary software or take advice from neighbouring churches. Change your strategy to reflect those growing abilities.
3. Recruit new people to the team as appropriate and change your strategy to reflect their abilities too.

Identity

5. Decide the kind of identity that your church wants to have.

Imagine you know nothing about McDonald's, and you see one of their adverts for the first time. There are images of a clown making children laugh, families biting into burgers and smiling at each other, and mouth-watering ingredients falling onto a tasty bun. You would assume this was the perfect place to take your children for a wholesome meal. This isn't the place to debate the merits of McDonald's food – it's enough for us to note that such companies spend literally millions of pounds promoting such images. Their 'corporate identity' is incredibly important.

Now think of the identity of your own church or denomination. What do outsiders really think about you? A handful of old people listening to boring sermons? Full of 'happy clappy' worshippers listening to choruses strummed on guitars? Only interested in saving people's souls? Irreconcilably divided over homosexuals or women bishops? Those images may be completely wide of the mark because they have never set foot in your church, but such impressions are important. As soon as someone suggests coming to your church, that may be what they immediately think of.

It might be worth conducting some kind of survey to discover what local people think. Often, if your church is active in the community, people hold two separate impressions in their heads – that your denomination is hopelessly divided at national level, but their local church is actually quite friendly. The results are likely to be quite illuminating and may help you decide how to promote your church over the next year to correct those misconceptions.

Then you might want to think about the kind of identity you'd like to promote. Much of this may depend on your type of church. Is yours an informal, family-friendly congregation with children's groups on Sundays? Or a youth-oriented church where radical discipleship and rave-style worship are emphasised? Or a more traditional congregation, where worship centres on the weekly Communion service? It might be a mixture of lots of things, especially if your church has different styles of worship at different services. But it might be worth settling on some kind of phrase that would sum up your church accurately to outsiders. Be honest: if your congregation are all pensioners, it may be difficult to sell yourself as a 'family' church, however much you might like it to be.

Promoting this identity will be useful in much of your communication. It may help you to decide on your priorities, to create a logo, or even to dictate the style of your communication. For instance, if you're aiming primarily at teenagers, it's better for your publicity to be via websites, e-mails, text messages and nightclub-style flyers.

How to do it:

1. Conduct a survey to find out what local people think about your church. This might involve talking to people in the streets or even delivering questionnaires to households. People are often wary of strangers knocking on their doors these days, but this method could lead to some interesting face-to-face conversations. Ask open questions such as: 'What do you know about our church?', 'What impression do you have of the people who go to services?', 'Do you know about any of the other activities it runs?'

2. Collate the results and discover where the misconceptions are. If appropriate, resolve to concentrate communications on those areas. If, for instance, people mistakenly think your church is full of older people, take every opportunity to use photos of younger people in your publicity.

3. Think about the kind of identity you would like your church to have. Try to sum it up in a short phrase you can use to inform your publicity material. You may be able to use the phrase on publicity material itself (e.g.: 'A church at the heart of its community', or 'A friendly, informal, family church').

6. Create a logo or update your existing one to reflect your church's identity.

One way of promoting your church's preferred identity is through a logo. We're all familiar with logos without necessarily realising it – the visual symbol or typeface used consistently to denote a company, organisation, group or institution. Think about Coca-Cola and a particular type-face, as well as particular colours, will spring to mind. The idea, of course, is twofold: (i) to make that particular brand more widely known by plastering a recognisable logo everywhere; and (ii) to associate that brand with a modern font, aspirational symbol or smiling face to make you think that consuming that brand will make you happier or more satisfied.

It might sound a little worldly to think about marketing the Church in the same way. But there's nothing new about logos or brands. Old-fashioned family crests, which used lions, crowns and mottos to denote bravery or royal con-nections were a way of promoting individuals as part of a family 'brand'. And, as Christians, we are already associated with one of the best-known logos in the world – the cross. We mustn't, of course, fall into the trap of promoting our church as something it isn't: we must remain honest in our marketing. But there's nothing wrong with using modern methods to do so.

Businesses spend thousands of pounds getting the look of their logo right, to try to make sure they communicate the right image. There are well-known examples of companies scrapping a logo or brand name to re-launch in a new way. Your church will not have those resources. But if you have a clear idea of the identity that you want to promote, creat-ing or revamping your logo might be one way to do so.

If your church decided it wanted to promote itself as a 'family-friendly, informal worshipping community', you could create a symbol to suggest precisely that – perhaps a simple image of a parent and child worshipping together. It could be used on noticeboards, letterheads, the parish magazine and so on. It would act as a visual reminder of the message that you want to get across.

Many churches already have some kind of logo. It might help to look carefully at it. Your 'logo' might be a line drawing of the church building itself. This isn't necessarily a bad thing – it helps people recognise that your literature originated from a building they may see regularly. But it may simply reinforce the message that 'the church' merely represents the building, rather than the people inside it. Or perhaps your building looks old fashioned, despite the fact that your style of worship is actually quite modern. Is that the image you want to promote?

Using an architectural feature of your church in your logo may help people to identify which church you represent, but it is possible to do so in a modern way. The logo below, for instance, took advantage of the fact that this church is the only one in the entire city to have a spire – a spire used by sailors as a landmark in navigation. Yet it managed to use an image of the spire in a modern way, and with a modern typeface, to communicate the modern worship styles used by the congregation.

St Jude's
Southsea

You could show your church's commitment to the local community, or its geographical location, by incorporating recognisable elements of the neighbourhood into the design, such as high-rise flats in an inner city:

Or you could use the name of your church to create something like these:

The constraints of this book make it difficult to show here the effect that different colours can have. See www. getyourchurchnoticed.com for examples of use of colour.

Be careful, however, about incorporating Christian symbols into your design. Logos that include a cross, dove, fire or fish symbol could, of course, denote any Christian organisation worldwide. Not only that, but symbols that might mean something to Christians, such as a dove or a fish, may mean nothing to outsiders. If it's not completely clear, they may assume you keep birds or sell fish.

Beware also the temptation to include too much in your logo. Your credo should be 'the simpler, the better'. You can imagine an over-active imagination producing the following for a worldwide Christian organisation:

World Outreach All Day Mission

The choice of typeface or font that you use for the name of your church is also important. An antique, gothic typeface might suggest a very traditional church:

St David's Church, Putney

Something more frivolous might suggest that your church knows how to have fun:

Glasgow Family Church

But, in general, a relaxed, modern typeface is probably what you are after:

Church of the Good Shepherd, Birmingham

One mistake some churches make is to hold a competition among the congregation to come up with a logo – or to hold a vote to see which one they like best. This can be a mistake for two reasons. First, getting any group to agree on something usually means a compromise, but logos work best when they involve one clear, simple idea. Secondly, this is an area of some expertise. Just as you wouldn't necessarily invite the whole congregation to have a go at re-tiling the church roof, you shouldn't necessarily allow them all to decide your logo. Do hire a graphic designer, unless you are fortunate enough to have one in your congregation already.

How to do it:

1. Decide on the church identity that you would like to promote (see Idea 5).
2. Think of what makes your church particularly special and recognisable: its location, an architectural feature, its tradition, its involvement in the local community.
3. Hire a graphic designer (unless you have one in the congregation) and instruct them to produce a design taking into account your answers to both 1 and 2. Ask them to include the name of the church into the design using a suitable font.
4. Ask them to produce several possibilities, and present them to your church leadership. Choose the one that most closely fits with your requirements.

5. Ask the graphic designer to produce designs for a series of items, including letterheads, a parish magazine, a weekly leaflet and a website, to see how the logo would be used in each.
6. Make sure the graphic designer gives you copies of the logo in as many formats as you will need (jpg, tif, EPS files; colour and black and white) to include it on the literature produced by your church.

7. Use your new logo on all church literature.

You may, of course, have a church logo that you already use and are happy with. You may have several. Sometimes, because different people – paid and voluntary – within your church community produce different items of literature, you may discover that what one person uses to symbolise your church differs from another.

Consistency is important for several reasons:

(i) You want to promote your church's identity in the way that you have agreed. Seeing the same logo each time will reinforce this message.

(ii) You want people to look at any item produced by your church and relate it to your worshipping community. Having the same logo on a piece of literature posted through their letterbox as the one on the church noticeboard will help this process.

(iii) You also want to ensure that every piece of church literature is of a high standard. The chances are that the logo designed for you by a professional will be better than one designed by an enthusiastic amateur.

However, the practical aspects of this need to be thought about. You may be fortunate enough to have a church office that produces every item of literature, in which case it should be fairly simple to adopt a common style. But if not, there may be all sorts of people producing orders of service, weekly leaflets, evangelistic pamphlets and posters. This is where your communications team can come into its own, agreeing some kind of common 'look' to all items of literature (perhaps even always using the same typeface for all text, as well as the church logo!), and ensuring consistency.

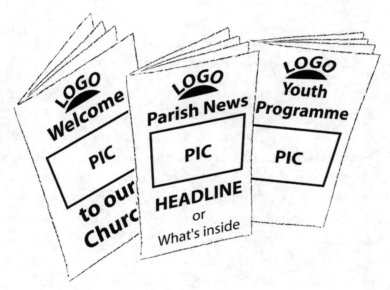

How to do it:

1. Create a new logo (see Idea 6) or – if you are happy with your existing one – make sure that you have copies of it in colour, black and white, large and small, in as many formats as may be necessary.

2. Make sure everyone who has responsibility for creating church literature has copies of the logo.
3. Agree some basic ground rules for using it: will it always be placed in the top left or top right corner? What font should you use for accompanying text? Will you always print church literature on a particular colour paper to reinforce consistency, or will you all use the same professional printers?
4. Use the church logo for internal displays within the church, add it to your external noticeboard: use it wherever the name of your church appears.

8. Create a joint identity/logo with nearby churches of all denominations to reflect your unity.

Non-churchgoers often think the Church has a bewildering number of different denominations and styles. This perceived lack of unity among churches communicates its own message to non-churchgoers, one that can easily cloud the gospel message. For some, it may be a convenient excuse to cite disagreements among Christians as a reason for not considering the faith, but for others it may be a genuine problem.

One way to show unity among Christians in your area is, of course, to make sure you work together as often as possible. Many Churches Together groups in the UK do run joint projects and hold joint services. However, such unity is not necessarily obvious to those who aren't involved with church.

It may therefore be appropriate to promote a joint identity in the form of a joint logo – at least for those things that churches in your area do together. Some kind of 'Churches Together in [name of community]' or 'Christians in [name of town]' logo would be good. The symbol might reflect the fact that Christians of different backgrounds are working together:

If the aim is to work towards doing even more together, this is a logo that can be used more and more – and hopefully might become recognised in its own right.

How to do it:

1. In the same way as the creation of a church logo, it's good to hire a graphic designer, giving him or her a specific brief.
2. In this case, the logo needs to be agreed by all the churches involved. That can, of course, take time.
3. Make sure those involved with communications and publicity in each church have access to the logo and can use it on items of literature that promote joint events.
4. Working together on a joint logo might help communications teams in different churches to get to know each

other better. It might lead to plans to work together on other things – perhaps a welcome pack that publicises all the churches equally (see Idea 39), or an ecumenical newsletter (see Idea 62). Look out for other opportunities when you can present the churches in your neighbourhood as united.

Building (External)

9. Create a more modern look to the outside of your church building.

Like it or not, your church building will communicate something about your church. If yours is a medieval Anglican parish church, people will expect worship to be traditional. If it is a 1980s concrete building, they may think services are more contemporary. Of course, if windows are smashed or boarded up, doors locked, and brickwork falling off, that also communicates something – a neglected building suggests a moribund church community or even that the church has closed altogether!

Maintaining church buildings isn't easy, of course, and modernising them is even more difficult. Whole books have been written on funding and designing such projects. It's enough here to suggest that, if you want your church to be promoted as an attractive venue for the whole community, what it looks like on the outside may not be helping. Repairing the church roof might not seem like a vital communication task, but it might be just as important as designing a website.

One thing that may help is the use of glass to enable people to see more easily what's going on inside. Many older church buildings are made from hefty amounts of stone or brick, with stained-glass windows and huge, wooden doors. Even an enterprising passer-by would be hard-pressed to discover what was happening inside without crossing the threshold. Why not make it easier for them – as well as making the church itself lighter and more airy – by incorporating more glass into the structure? That's assuming that what goes on inside is worth seeing, of course! Passers-by should be able to see activities and events that might help to challenge some preconceptions of what church is like.

How to do it:

1. There's not space here to detail the kind of work needed for a major church renovation project, but the first step might be to look at what other churches in your locality, or in similar areas in different parts of the country, have done.
2. You may need to commission some kind of feasibility study to see what's possible.
3. Liaise with an architect and ask him or her to produce some designs. In discussions, bear in mind that you are aiming to produce a modern-looking building or extension that looks accessible. Glass may be helpful so passers-by can see inside.
4. There may be several stages of planning permission – local authority and church – that you need to get through.
5. Obtain quotes for the work to be done. Hire a construction firm.
6. You will probably need to raise some money to get the work done. Depending on how old your church is, you may be able to apply to various grant-giving bodies such as English Heritage or the Historic Churches' Preservation Society.
7. Use methods such as press releases (see Idea 74), not just to help you raise the money, but also to advertise the fact that work has been completed.

Further resources:

For more information on the restoration of historic churches, see: www.english-heritage.org.uk and www.

historicchurches.org.uk. For more information about fundraising ideas, see: www.fundraising.co.uk or www. churchcare.co.uk

10. Lobby your local authority to create a sign identifying your church from the nearest main roads.

All your careful efforts to communicate events and activities will be no use if no one can actually find your church. Don't assume everyone knows where it is, even if it is in the centre of your community. They may never have looked at your building properly, or they might be confused about which church is which.

One way to help people find your church is to ask for road signs to be put up, guiding people from the nearest main roads to your church building. Even if someone never passes your building, if they pass a road sign featuring your church's name, they may sub-consciously take in where to find it.

How to do it:

1. Apply to your local authority for a road sign to be erected on your nearest main roads. This should normally be put in writing and addressed to your authority's highways department.
2. If your church is a historic one, it may qualify for brown 'tourist information' signs, which can direct drivers from the nearest motorway or A-road. This also involves a

letter to the highways department, stressing its historic credentials.

11. Keep your church building open as often as possible during the day.

Keeping church buildings open during the day for visitors is a great way of communicating that churches are welcoming places. Those who might feel cautious about crossing the threshold on a Sunday can creep in unnoticed during the week, perhaps to spend time in prayer, or just out of curiosity.

Sadly, many congregations these days feel they can't take the risk of doing so because of the possibility of theft or vandalism. This is an understandable reaction, particularly if valuable items have gone missing. But research in this area seems to suggest that it is the 'fortresses' that are locked up every day and night (apart from a couple of hours on Sunday morning) that attract the most attention from vandals and thieves. Buildings that are used for activities throughout the day or in the evening are less likely to be targeted, as thieves and vandals can't be sure whether someone is just about to arrive or leave.

Rural churches, cathedrals, historic churches and those on well-established tourist trails are more likely to be visited during the day. But that doesn't mean the urban or suburban church won't attract some visitors. Try it for a limited period initially, perhaps with some volunteers available, offering coffee or a chat, and you might be surprised who wanders in.

How to do it:

1. Consider your diary of regular activities during the week. Might it be possible to open the church while others are in the building, while your parish office is manned, or while your caretaker is working inside?
2. If you are worried about the security implications, consider whether some volunteers could be available to talk to people, perhaps for a couple of hours each day (see Ideas 12 and 16).
3. If you are going to open the church, do make sure you have some visual displays, welcome packs or other resources available so that people can find out more about what the church does throughout the week (see Ideas 39–42 and 43–46).
4. Make sure that people *know* that the church is open, perhaps by posting a leaflet through people's letterboxes or issuing a press release (see Idea 74).

Further resources:

The Open Churches Trust seeks to find ways to keep church buildings open across the UK. See: www.openchurchestrust. org.uk for details.

12. Create a 'welcome/the church is open' sign and place it outside where passers-by will see it.

If your church is already open during the day, one simple thing you can do to let people know is to place a sign outside the front door. The combination of an old-fashioned building with few windows and a heavy, wooden door often makes it difficult to tell from the outside whether a church is actually open or not. It's not a mistake that a shopkeeper would make. Something as simple as this could double or treble the number of visitors coming into your building.

How to do it:

1. Buy or create an 'A-frame' noticeboard – one that can display posters on both sides and is self-supporting.

2. Create colourful, welcoming posters to go on both sides. If possible, use your church logo, photos of congregation members (perhaps lighting a candle) or other images. Include, in large letters, wording such as: '[name of church] is open for prayer and reflection'.

3. Find a good location for it. If your church opens straight onto the street, it should be possible to place the board immediately outside the front door, but not where it obstructs the pathway. If your church has a churchyard, make sure the notice goes outside the entrance to your church's grounds – in other words, public space, not private space. If that entrance is on a quiet street, you may even want to find the nearest main road and put a sign there (with the permission of the local authority) perhaps with an arrow showing the direction people need to take.

4. Recruit someone (the verger or caretaker, perhaps) to put out the board each morning and bring it in at the end of the day.

5. Do also make sure that the church is open whenever the board is out!

13. Decorate the outside of church, not just the inside.

Imagine a special occasion in your church's calendar. Depending on the type of church you go to, it's likely that an army of church cleaners, flower arrangers or banner-makers will be called in to make the inside of your church look as nice as possible. No doubt the wedding couple, retiring minister or baptism family will be impressed.

But it's quite possible that the outside of your building might look just as drab as normal. Why not make an effort to spruce up its external appearance to tell the rest of the world that something special is happening? That might involve using balloons, lights or streamers – anything to brighten it up.

But why just confine this to special occasions? Why not cultivate window boxes, flowers or plants outside your church building? Why not tie balloons to the railings outside your church each time you have a family service? Such things suggest that your congregation cares about its appearance and wants to make a contribution to what the local neighbourhood looks like. It's another sign that your congregation is not inward-looking.

How to do it:

1. Decide what kind of decoration would be most appropriate for your church, given its location and size, whether it has a churchyard or not, and the type of building.
2. Recruit some congregation members to do the work. This might be a good role for frustrated gardeners who might not have much of a garden at home. Or, if necessary, suggest that flower arrangers and banner-makers might like to decorate the outside of the church rather than the inside for one week a month.
3. Keep regularly maintaining whatever it is that you choose to do. Wilted flowers, dead plants or burst balloons may communicate the opposite message from the one you want to get across.

14. Drape a banner from the spire/roof to advertise special events.

When churches put on some kind of special event – a children's holiday club or a mission week – organisers often wrestle for hours about how they can publicise it, without thinking about one obvious resource they could use: the building itself. Why not drape some kind of banner from it when you want *everyone* to notice what's happening? Not every organisation has a dedicated building that it can use to publicise events and activities in this way. Some would no doubt be envious of a 100-foot spire that can be seen across town!

Apart from anything else, it does mean that if the church is, say, teaming with teenagers, passers-by don't have to look very far to discover why. This is really a once-a-year method to attract attention to something very significant. If your church was to employ this method every week, passers-by may become used to it.

How to do it:

1. It is possible, of course, to create a banner yourself. Try to resist this temptation, as – unless your congregation includes artists and graphic designers – it may look amateur. As this is such a high-profile method of publicity, it's important that it looks as good as possible. Hire professional banner-makers to do it for you.

2. Use the same logos, images and typefaces that you are using in your written literature to advertise the same event. That means people will connect the information

BUILDING (EXTERNAL)   61

that may have been pushed through their letterbox with the building the banner is hanging from.

3. Find a way of attaching the banner to the spire or church roof.

4. It's possible that the unfurling of the banner itself might be a big enough news event to get the local newspaper or TV station out to cover it. If so, use the opportunity to publicise the holiday club or mission that your banner is advertising.

Building (Internal)

15. Redesign your church's entrance or foyer to make it look more attractive.

Church architecture can be a matter of huge debate. What might look modern, spacious and elegant to one person can look cold and functional to another. What looks reassuringly traditional to me could seem dark and gloomy to you. Confusingly, non-churchgoers often say they prefer churches to look like what they think a church *should* look like – wooden pews, stained-glass windows and lofty ceilings. Perhaps they feel more comfortable with the stereotype. Yet take them to a modern church building with better facilities, comfy seats and effective heating and they may be pleasantly surprised.

Any entrance or foyer will create a good or bad first impression as people cross the threshold. Think of all the thought that goes into creating a welcoming reception area for a large business. Too often, our church's entrance can be anything but welcoming. There may be several large, thick wooden doors to negotiate. If you've never been inside a church before, this can be intimidating. Glass doors help people to see what's inside before they go in.

Our entrances often end up cluttered with tatty notices, old-fashioned tea urns or piles of hymn books. This will all communicate something to the casual observer. There are umpteen books on the market about 'de-cluttering' people's homes. Perhaps we should apply the same principles to churches. It involves taking realistic decisions about whether something is likely to be used in future, throwing away old things and finding effective storage solutions for things that need to be kept.

Your church entrance may need to be re-designed to cater for the casual visitor. That might actually involve some structural work to your building, perhaps creating a 'foyer' with displays of church activities, a bookstall and an attractive display of items for people to browse before entering the worship area itself. Or you may need to create some space for visual displays of church activities (see Ideas 43–46).

How to do it:

1. Consider the entrance to your church. Are your doors intimidating, or is your entrance too cluttered? What are the first impressions a visitor might have? Recruit a friendly non-church person to help you assess this.
2. De-clutter the area. Be ruthless. Even if you decide to keep some items, find somewhere else in the church building to store them.
3. Sometimes well-meaning churchgoers will donate items like an old bookcase to help display books and leaflets.

Learn to say 'no' to such items: if someone doesn't want it in their house, why should it be acceptable for church?

4. What steps could you take to make it look more welcoming? Glass doors? Visual displays? A 'foyer' area? Some comfortable chairs? Pot plants? A 'reception' desk with a volunteer who is willing to chat?

16. Ensure there is a rota of people who can be discreetly available in church if anyone needs information or prayer.

If your church is open during the week, you may attract all sorts of visitors. Some want time and space to be quiet and reflect. Others may want to chat with someone. It's good to have those who can tell the difference discreetly available in your church whenever it is open. If you can put together a rota of volunteers, it could help you to create a welcoming ethos.

Such 'church-sitters' might be available to help visitors discover more about the history of the church, provide prayer resources, offer hot drinks, or even offer to pray with them. But they should also allow people the time and space to spend a few minutes in private prayer and reflection if that's what they want. Their secondary role, of course, might be one of security.

In one church that was regularly open to the public on Sunday afternoons, one of the church-sitters deliberately strolled around *outside* the building, gazing intently at the architecture. It helped to convey to passers-by that there was something interesting to look at!

How to do it:

1. Identify people who might be able to devote an hour or two to 'church-sitting' during the week. They may be able to combine this with another activity if they are caretakers, church cleaners or flower-arrangers.

2. Give them some training on how to offer discreet help to visitors. This might involve showing them where relevant church literature is kept, telling them about Alpha or Emmaus courses, giving them an up-to-date diary of church activities or giving them a refresher course in the history of your church. It could also involve training in praying with those who are distressed.

3. If you attract sufficient visitors, consider whether you could offer visitors tea and coffee for free.

4. Organise a rota, and let people know when they will be required. For security reasons, there should always be at least two people available when the church is open.

5. Examine whether you can organise the layout of the church in such a way as to accommodate all types of visitors: for instance, tables, chairs and church literature at the back of church, so some can talk over tea and coffee; and perhaps a screen between them and the worship area so others who want peace and quiet won't be disturbed.

17. Create a coffee shop or bookshop within your church.

One logical extension to the idea of having a church open with refreshments available, is actually to open a coffee shop within the building. Charging money for drinks and snacks opens up the church to regulations governing café premises. But in a busy town or city centre church, making the serving of refreshments more 'professional' may actually entice shoppers inside.

Equally, a proper bookshop may be another way of attracting visitors. Selling Christian books, music, newspapers and gifts, of course, has the added advantage that the products themselves will communicate something about the faith. If you have few or no other Christian bookshops in the area, you may also attract Christians from other churches. These days, the philosophy behind bookshops seems to be to let people flop into armchairs and devour whole chapters while they sip coffee. Wouldn't it be great to have our churches full of people reading Christian books?

There are several ways a church might do this, but the best way might be to work in partnership with a firm that already does this – a national chain of Christian bookshops or a national coffee shop chain. As the landlord, you could even insist in a lease that the coffee and snacks sold in the café were Fairtrade or ethically sourced. But your church wouldn't have to get involved in the minutiae of stock-taking or health and safety requirements.

If that's not possible, it might be possible for the church to employ a coffee shop or bookshop manager with experience in the café or retail sector. It's tempting to think that volunteers could do the same kind of job. They could, but do think seriously about this. The initial vision could become diluted, and you could end up with poorly trained volunteers offering small numbers of visitors sub-standard coffee or dog-eared, second-hand books. This could easily communicate the wrong message to a casual visitor.

How to do it:

1. Research thoroughly the existing provision of cafés, bookshops and Christian bookshops in your area. Would there be demand for another one?
2. Contact national chains of Christian bookshops and coffee shops. Would they be interested in locating or relocating a branch within your church? What incentives could you offer them?
3. Investigate the possibility of employing your own coffee shop or bookshop manager, and the set-up costs of buying the right equipment, the right stock of books, cash tills, comfy seating and so on. Look at the likely initial losses and potential profits of such an operation. Is it viable? Take advice from those who have set up businesses before.
4. If you decide that you can only do this with volunteers, think carefully about how you can ensure a sufficient level of quality in the finished product to make it worthwhile as a tool of mission. Avoid the temptation to cut corners on the training of volunteers, the purchase of appropriate equipment and the regular updating of stock.
5. However you end up creating a bookshop or coffee shop, do make sure that the initial vision isn't lost in the desire to make profits.

18. Think about what your seating area communicates to visitors.

If you succeed in getting new people inside your church building, you've won half the battle. But allowing new-comers to feel welcomed and accepted into the church community is often vital before they find out more about the faith. 'Belonging' often comes before 'believing'. Hence the popularity of courses like Alpha, in which people are welcomed without having to sign up to Christianity. One thing that may communicate something to visitors – probably sub-consciously – is the way in which the seating is arranged. This applies whether or not they actually stay for a worship service.

If your seating is in straight lines, all facing the front, this communicates that your church practises a 'performance' model, as in a theatre or cinema. In this model, a celebrant or worship leader or preacher 'performs' at the front of church, and the rest of the congregation watch or sing or speak as essentially passive participants. If your seating is in a semi-circle or a full circle around a central, shared area, it suggests that your church is more interested in participation by the whole worshipping community. It's easier to do this if you can see other people's faces rather than the backs of their heads.

This isn't dependent on the style of worship your church uses. Guitar-based worship bands and charismatic preach-ers can be just as guilty of falling into the 'performance' mode as Anglo-Catholic priests for whom the celebration of the Eucharist is paramount. Equally, both styles of church-manship can lend themselves to true participation by the

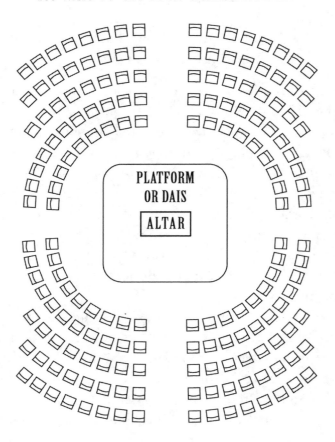

whole body of worshippers. It's the difference between worship being done *to* a congregation and worship being done *by* a congregation.

How you enable congregation members to participate properly in public acts of worship is another matter, which is explored more fully in literature about worship. But, from a communication point of view, if your church wants visitors to think that worship is something done jointly by the whole congregation, the layout of your seating may be important.

How to do it:

1. Examine the kind of worship you offer in Sunday and midweek services. Is it truly participative, or does it tend towards the 'performance' model? Is this the message you would like to convey?
2. Think about re-organising your seating in a semi-circle or full circle around a central altar or shared area. This may involve some re-ordering of your church building, moving the altar or replacing your chairs.
3. Don't assume that you can't do this just because you have pews. They can be moved into new positions.
4. You might like to re-organise the seating for a trial period, as this is the kind of change that is sometimes difficult for a congregation to get used to.

19. Create the right ambience inside the church for prayer and reflection.

If your church building is fairly traditional, your stained-glass windows, soaring architecture and sense of peace should help visitors genuinely meet with God. But in other churches, more aids to worship might be necessary to help people with private spiritual reflection.

It's difficult to generalise as people have different spiritualities. But it's no coincidence that lighting a candle is a popular way of symbolising that a prayer has been said. Many churches have simple votive candle stands to encourage visitors to do this. If some are already lit before a visitor enters church, it helps to give them a focus for their reflections. In some churches, the aroma of incense helps to suggest the fragrance of prayers sent heavenwards.

Perhaps your church is a more modern building, without stained-glass windows or impressive architecture. It's still possible to create an ambience to help people engage spiritually. Maybe you could have a CD player playing Christian worship songs or choral works quietly. Perhaps you could have images depicting icons, Bible verses or prayers projected onto a wall via a PowerPoint projector. What about using part of the building as a 'prayer corner', with the chance to write prayers on Post-it notes or in an intercessions book that will be used during worship? Or what about encouraging them simply to 'be still' with God?

All of these things will stimulate the senses and encourage people to engage spiritually. But they will also communicate the fact that your church takes spiritual things seriously, and is interested in helping visitors to meet with God. One thing that can be off-putting is frequent requests all around the building for money – for the roof appeal, general church funds, special projects or even to light a candle. That communicates that you are more interested in the contents of your visitors' wallets than their spiritual lives.

How to do it:

1. Consider the ways in which the spiritual life of visitors is catered for within your church at the moment.
2. Consider which methods mentioned above might complement what you do already – a prayer corner or a votive candle stand; a CD of worship music or a book of intercessions.
3. If you have some kind of prayer corner or book of intercessions in which needy people can request prayer, do

make sure you say those prayers in a relatively private way – not in the main Sunday service.

4. Consider whether anything detracts from the spiritual experience – the noise from meetings and activities, requests for money or the chatter of church cleaners.

5. Try out a few different ideas and decide which of them seems to be most effective. Ask visitors for feedback about what they find the most helpful.

20. Create a prayer guide to help visitors engage spiritually.

Another way of helping visitors to engage with their spirituality is to give them some literature they can use. A prayer guide might contain helpful verses or prayers, or suggestions on how to pray, which can be used in a moment of quiet reflection. Some visitors to your church may never have prayed before, or pray rarely. Giving them words to express how they feel can be helpful.

This guide needn't be long. It might simply be a card or a bookmark, piles of which you might scatter around the building. You might even let visitors take such guides away with them.

How to do it:

1. Assess what written material you already have in your church building to help visitors engage spiritually. If necessary, update it.

2. If you regularly host visitors, consider a prayer guide as a serious option. Churches are often good at providing

information about their building, but less good at providing easy ways for visitors to engage with their spirituality.

3. Place such cards or bookmarks in your pews, your lady chapel, in front of your votive candle stand, or other places where visitors might choose to spend a quiet moment.

Locations

21. Think about different places for your congregation to meet.

You probably agree that 'the church' is really the local group of Christians, rather than the building they meet in. You probably also feel comfortable meeting with a group you know well. Yet that's probably not how it looks from the outside. To most non-churchgoers, 'church' means the imposing-looking building that they would rather not enter. And they feel uncomfortable stepping over the threshold to try to join what seems like an exclusive 'club' if they don't know the rules or any of the other members.

Some of the ideas in this book are to do with making the church building itself look more welcoming, but there is an important strand of modern Christian thinking that suggests that it's better to 'take church to where people are'. If people feel more comfortable worshipping with small groups whom they already know and in a place where they feel comfortable, why ask them to go elsewhere? Some of this kind of thinking will be examined in the following sections.

The same principle can be applied to your whole

congregation as well as small groups within it. If some people feel intimidated stepping over your threshold, why not move the whole congregation to another building occasionally? If it can be done in partnership with the organisation that owns the building, so much the better. A worship service in a school to mark its centenary, to which all pupils have been invited, could be very valuable. The fact that you're happy to meet in a location that is not an official church helps to communicate the fact that 'the church' is actually its members. It also suggests that you are flexible and not tied to a specific location.

Equally, if you choose to hold your service in a community centre on a nearby estate every once in a while, it sends a message to those residents. It says that your church is interested in making its services accessible to them. Of course, you have to be careful that you aren't treading on the toes of another congregation already based there.

How to do it:

1. Think about the community that your church serves. Are there parts of it that might benefit from you occasionally holding church services there?
2. Think also about some of the other institutions in the locality. Could you join forces with them and hold an occasional service on their turf for a special occasion?
3. Make sure you publicise your presence as widely as you can within the local area. Whether people come or not, the fact that you are there communicates an important message.
4. When you meet elsewhere, use something that helps to

identify who you are, such as a banner with your church's name and logo on to drape over the entrance. Passers-by will also take away a valuable message about the nature of your church.

22. Plant a new congregation in a part of your neighbourhood that may not be served by a church.

If you've successfully met in a different part of town a few times, it might be time to think about a church plant. The idea of starting a new congregation may seem intimidating, but research has proved that this is one of the best ways of the Church as a whole growing. This is especially true if you have a large congregation. In a church of more than 200, people may well come and go without you noticing, making real discipleship and genuine growth difficult. But two churches with 100 people can expand further before the law of diminishing returns takes hold. Not just that, but having two separate congregations allows more of those people to be in leadership roles, giving them valuable experience.

Whole books have, of course, been written on this subject; it's certainly true that the convenience of having a church on people's doorsteps makes it easier for them to consider coming. And the fact that your new congregation is likely to be meeting in a school or community centre can make it less intimidating.

Of course, before you take such a step, it's worth consulting with other churches already operating in the area. Not only do you not want to tread on their toes, but you might find that an ecumenical approach to church-planting works even better. A brand new, ecumenical church for a specific neighbourhood communicates that the church in your area is growing, that Christians care enough for local residents to start a new congregation for them, and that Christians are united in their witness. This kind of approach is particularly valuable in places where whole estates or new towns are being built. If no church exists at the moment, a new inter-denominational church can be created from scratch.

Often such church plants, by virtue of their meeting place, tend to be more informal than their 'parent' church. There are no old church buildings to preserve and there is no history of worshipping in a particular way. They are often smaller too, which can make them easier to join. Sometimes this informal, more experimental way of worshipping can make some Christians feel uncomfortable. Before long, they may decide they want a building of their own with all the responsibility that goes with it. Of course, a church building does communicate the presence of Christians in the midst of that neighbourhood, but it's important to remember that not having a 'proper' building has advantages of its own.

How to do it:

1. Consider the size of your church and the area it serves. Could you identify part of your congregation who could start a new church in a specific locality nearby? Do enough of them live in that area for them to identify with the people who live there?

2. Identify who might lead such a group. Talk to them privately to see if they would be willing to do so. It's important to know who the leaders might be, and for them to pray about it, before going any further.

3. Talk to other nearby churches about the idea. You may be surprised to discover that they are thinking along similar lines. Consider creating an ecumenical church.

4. Consider where such a group could meet regularly. You will need to find somewhere that could be a long-term home for at least a few years. A community centre or school hall could be ideal.

5. Introduce the idea to your congregation. Ask for volunteers who feel God is calling them to serve that community. Or, if your house groups or Bible study groups meet on a geographical basis, suggest that a few groups in that locality might want to consider forming the core group of the church plant.

6. Publicise the existence of the new church among the specific community you are trying to reach.

7. Delegate authority to the leaders of the new church – under the authority of your denomination. If the 'mother' church interferes too much in the running of the 'daughter' church, then the latter's leadership are not being given a chance to grow and experiment for themselves.

Further resources:

For more details about the Anglican Church Planting Initiative, see: www.acpi.org.uk

23. Think about creating church plants or cell groups that are not bound by where people live, but by shared interests.

In the UK, and particularly the Church of England, congregations tend to be organised by geography. Each church has its own 'parish', and most worshippers live in that area, unless they deliberately choose to travel further to go somewhere with a specific style of worship.

But think for a minute about the average, non-church-going family. These families may live in a suburban street where they know none of their neighbours well. They may know few other people who live nearby. Their social circles may include their workplaces, which are several miles away, the gym, tennis club, sailing club, model-railway club or amateur dramatics group. All of these places bring together people who don't necessarily live in the same area. Many people, therefore, make friends with networks of others who share their interests. They would drive across the city to see friends from the golf club, but wouldn't speak to their next-door neighbour.

It's this kind of network culture that the Church finds it hard to break into, as our models tend to be still based on geography. Bishop Graham Cray and a working group of the Church of England identified this problem in their report *Mission-Shaped Church* and suggested that one way to overcome it was by greater use of non-geographical cell churches. Mark Greene and the London Institute of Contemporary Christianity have also consistently emphasised the importance of evangelism in the workplace, as we spend so much time there.

Part of the thinking behind 'cell church' is to tap into these network cultures by creating groups of Christians who meet in such places. We may know other Christians at work, but rarely get together to pray or talk about work issues. We may meet other Christian parents at the school gates with whom we have much in common, but we may belong to different congregations and so rarely swap ideas. Meeting as a 'cell group' for Bible study, prayer and mutual support may seem like an additional burden for Christians who may already be overwhelmed by meetings. What about meeting in such a way *instead* of meeting in our current Bible study groups?

Meeting with others who share the same interests means you can relate to each other better. You may all know that the manager is a bully or the secretary is difficult to get on with, so it's easier to pray about them. But there is also an important message being communicated to others by doing this. At the moment, your workmates may have no idea there are any Christians in their office or factory. It may surprise them to discover that a group meets together regularly in the lunch hour to read the Bible and pray. Meeting in a relatively high-profile way may help to counter any suggestion that Christianity is on the decline. Meeting more privately, in people's homes in the evenings, may not achieve this.

Not only that, but – crucially – it's much easier for non-churchgoers to talk to their workmates about spiritual issues, ask for prayer or even join in meetings than it would be for them to cross the threshold of a church. It's a way of bringing 'church' to people in places where they already feel comfortable. And, for us, it's a good way of breaking down the subconscious divide we create between the sacred (what we do on a Sunday) and the secular (what we do for the rest of the week). It brings our faith into the centre of our day-to-day lifestyle, which is usually a good way of making our outreach more effective.

One example may help us to understand the nature of the society we live in. A pastor regularly worked out at a gym, and began to chat to other regulars – initially about working out, but gradually about other issues too. When one of their number was tragically killed at an early age, his friends at the gym didn't quite know what to do. Perhaps they didn't feel they knew him well enough to go to the funeral. The pastor offered to lead a memorial service right there in the gym, where the man who had died had spent so much of his time. His friends from the gym felt more comfortable there, and the simple service was packed and very moving. 'Church' had been brought onto their patch.

How to do it:

1. Survey your congregation about their workplaces, leisure activities, shared-interest clubs, the schools their children go to etc. See if there are obvious places where enough Christians congregate to make a 'cell group' viable.

2. Members of your congregation may already know of other Christians in their workplace, their am-dram group or their sports club, perhaps from other nearby churches. Ask them to consider approaching these Christians to think about getting together regularly.

3. Find someone who is prepared to co-ordinate and lead each group. You may want to give these leaders some kind of training in how to do so, as this may be a very different scenario from meeting in someone's home in the evening.

4. Give each group some kind of loose structure (worship, Bible study, discussion about issues, prayer) that they can follow in their 'cells'. It needs to be something they can fall back on if necessary, but ideally the situation in which the group is meeting should dictate what the group does. For instance, a work group might want to look at how to live out their faith in the workplace. It should also be loose and informal enough for curious non-churchgoers to join without feeling like outsiders.

Further resources:

For information on cell churches, see the Anglican Cell Church Network at www.accn.org.uk, Cell Church UK at www.cellchurch.co.uk, and Fresh Expressions, a directory of new ways of being Church, at www.freshexpressions.org.uk To see the Church of England's report on *Mission-Shaped Church*, look at www.cofe.anglican.org. For information on being a Christian in the workplace, see: www.licc.org.uk

24. Hold a regular or occasional open-air service.

Just as meeting up for prayer and Bible study in the workplace or sports club helps to raise the profile of Christians in your communities, so does meeting outdoors occasionally. When you worship in your church building, you might as well be invisible to most passers-by. Unless your singing or your worship band is pretty loud, people may not even realise that a service is in progress.

The occasional service outdoors can help non-churchgoers realise that a genuinely committed worshipping community exists locally. Meeting in the local park, the local football ground, or even just outside your church building, if appropriate, will make people stop and take notice. In the 1980s, there was a trend for 'Make Way' marches – Christians walking along local streets, singing praise songs and waving banners. While this undoubtedly raised the profiles of churches, the act of 'marching' led some to wonder what the Christians were protesting about. Our tradition of 'carnival' has largely been lost, and most people only march when they have something to complain about. It normally takes a lot of colourful costumes and face-paint to convince UK audiences that you are actually celebrating.

Any outdoor service has to be planned well, and shouldn't necessarily be a replica of your normal indoor services. You are hoping to appeal to passers-by who may only be watching for a few minutes, so any liturgy, sermon or prayers need to be kept short. Even lively worship songs may not engage passers-by as much as we might hope, as they won't be able to join in. The things that work best are visual – drama sketches, mime, visual aids, colourful costumes, face-paint, balloons and banners. Ideally, they should be things that intrigue passers-by, causing them to stop and wonder what is going on. Anything too direct will seem like preaching, and most non-churchgoers don't like to be preached at. Outdoor Communion services don't generally work well, as they seem exclusive. If worshippers are taking part in a ritual that others can't participate in, those passers-by will inevitably feel like outsiders.

How to do it:

1. Think of an appropriate occasion to hold an outdoor service. Summer is an obvious time. Christmas might seem appropriate, but it will be cold and people will be anxious to get Christmas shopping done. The only way this might work is to have a group singing Christmas carols inside a warm shopping centre.

2. Think of a suitable venue. Parks, shopping centres or school grounds may be good venues. Ideally, it should be somewhere where you will be seen by passers-by.

3. Make sure you plan the service carefully. If your worshippers will be standing throughout, it should be no longer than 45 minutes. Think of the visual elements of the service that might intrigue – but not preach at – passers-by. Keep any sermon short.

4. Think about what participants might wear. This might be an occasion for informality, colourful costumes and face-paint (which communicate a sense of fun) rather than cassocks, surplices and choir robes (which communicate something more solemn).

5. Publicise the event, not just among your congregation, but also within the community, using posters, press releases and leaflets. Make sure you also have some literature about your church with you on the day that can be given out to anyone who expresses interest.

6. Make sure you have a banner with your church's name and logo on it, so that passers-by can tell which church you are all from.

Further resources:

For details of books of drama sketches to be used in outdoor services, see: www.ridinglights.org or www.topcattheatre.com

25. Think of seasonal alternative locations.

It can help to have a suitable backdrop for seasonal celebrations or the re-telling of Bible stories. It helps us to get into the right mood for whatever it is that we're celebrating, or to appreciate what it must have been like in biblical times. Imagine someone telling the story of Jesus calming the storm while aboard a flimsy fishing boat, or telling the story of Moses crossing the Red Sea to people sat on a beach.

Perhaps one year, your Harvest service could take place in a farm setting, to give people a flavour of what it is that we are thanking God for. The sights and smells associated with a farm, and the way that food gets from the field to the table, might be a revelation to some urban dwellers. So much the better.

Holding a Christmas service in a cold, dirty farm shed might help to convey something of the sacrifice Jesus made by choosing to be born on earth in such a place. Gazing at pictures of a clean baby in freshly laundered whites in an immaculate Nativity painting doesn't quite convey the reality of the situation. Clearly, this could also be combined with some drama or role play based on the Nativity story. Real animals could even be used.

There are other possibilities. The concept of carrying a cross through a city centre on Good Friday is well established in some neighbourhoods. Taking that a step further and actually seeing someone being tied to a cross and raised into the air might help to ram home what Jesus went through. And Easter Sunday services often take place outdoors at daybreak, to emphasise the time of day that the discovery of Jesus' resurrection took place.

How to do it:

1. Think about the seasonal possibilities you have, and places you could meet within striking distance of your church building.
2. Liaise with the farmer, the city centre manager, local authorities or whoever you need to get permission from to stage your service. If possible, involve your hosts in the service.
3. Think about how you could role-play some of the stories you are trying to convey, using costumes, dramatic readings or mime.
4. Publicise the service in advance to members of your congregation and to the wider community, using posters, leaflets and press releases.

26. Liaise with your local pub landlord to hold an informal service there.

The local pub is the centre of many people's social lives. But many Christians rarely go near pubs, perhaps because they disapprove of excessive drinking, or have other ways to socialise. The drinker's sole experience of Christians in pubs may be Salvation Army collectors rattling their tins. But the fact that church and pub rarely come together can help to foster the notion that Christians disapprove of pub culture completely.

It's a shame as, apart from anything else, the pub is one place where people may lose their inhibitions and start talking about religion. Of course, this may take the form of arguments, usually starting with some cliché like: 'All religions lead to God.' But if there's no one there to correct such misconceptions, those ideas may become even more ingrained.

There have been some noble attempts to mix church and pub life – notably exchanges where the pub landlord (who may have some wisdom about the human condition) preaches at church and the vicar takes charge of the bar. There are some clergy who are happy to go regularly into pubs, either for informal chats with regulars, or formal question-and-answer sessions where drinkers can raise queries about faith in a friendly atmosphere.

As the name suggests, to become a regular involves going to the pub regularly, and engaging with others. This obviously takes time. It also involves being genuinely friendly, rather than starting up conversations merely to evangelise. Even if you happen to be the vicar, you may find that people don't welcome such directness. But it might be necessary for some of your congregation to become regulars before you can suggest holding a service in the pub.

But if you do, you might be surprised at the reaction, especially if you suggest a Christmas carol service. The advantage of carols is that many will already know the words, and so will feel happier joining in. A service including a few songs, a brief 'Thought for the Day'-type talk and a prayer is likely to be the most you can manage. By bringing 'church' to a place where people already feel comfortable, you have saved them the embarrassment of having to cross your threshold. Those who still have a vestige of Christian faith may be grateful for this.

How to do it:

1. Get to know the landlord of your local pub. This may involve regular visits by a group from your church over a long period. It might also involve your minister visiting the landlord regularly.
2. Get to know some of the regulars too. Be open about the fact that you are Christians, and happy to answer questions, but don't let the subject dominate the conversation constantly. Offer to pray (privately) for any needs they have.
3. Offer to hold a question-and-answer session about Christianity in the pub, if appropriate.
4. Suggest to the landlord that you hold a carol service or a short, informal service in the pub. Or suggest that you could relay a service from your church into the pub, using a video link or an audio link, which would allow drinkers to sing along with hymns, songs or carols.

External Noticeboards

27. Relocate your noticeboards so they can be seen more easily.

The noticeboard outside your church is probably the item of church communication seen by more people than anything else. Hundreds or thousands of people may walk or drive past it each day. Most people in your neighbourhood probably haven't met anyone from your church, so your noticeboard – and your church building – is one of the few clues that passers-by have to go on. Yours might be a young, vibrant congregation, but if you are meeting in a traditional church building with a tatty noticeboard, few might realise this.

Many churches don't use noticeboards to their full potential, by neglecting them, filling them with too much information or putting them in the wrong places. Look at the location of advertising billboards. They are usually placed where pedestrians and motorists can't avoid them – near traffic lights, busy junctions, outside tube stations or next to parks. Some may even be next to railway lines, solely to attract the attention of train passengers. Where are your church's noticeboards? They may be right next to the entrance to your church, which is the ideal place for churchgoers to notice them. But others who walk or drive past may never see them – perhaps there is a tree in the way, or they are too far away from the road to be any use.

Before you think about revamping your noticeboards, think about exactly where they should be to attract the most attention. Do think as well about whether you might need more than one noticeboard to cover all the various ways people approach your church. Some people might currently walk past the back of your church building every day without realising what it is.

How to do it:

1. Research the main thoroughfares around your church. Do motorists tend to approach from one specific direction? Is there a route that parents use to reach the local school that takes them past one end of your building? Is the supermarket next door used constantly?
2. Armed with your research, decide where might be the best place for your noticeboards, or suggest places where you might put extra ones to maximise the potential for people to see them.
3. Think also about the direction in which your noticeboards face. If your church is on a busy traffic junction, a board positioned parallel to the road might be invisible to any driver waiting at the traffic lights. But two boards positioned at 45-degree angles to the road would cover traffic waiting in both directions.
4. If you are happy with your existing noticeboards and think they compare well with others along the same street, consider relocating them. If you feel they need a revamp, consult the following ideas (28–32) beforehand.

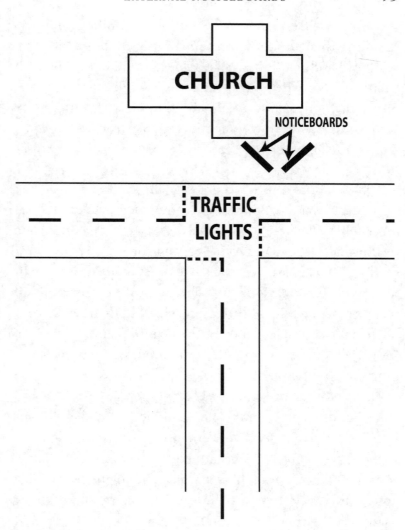

28. Revamp your noticeboards to suggest a more vibrant congregation.

Walk along the street your church is on. What attracts your attention? If there are shops, you'll see colourful posters in the windows, showing images of happy, smiling shoppers sampling their produce. Perhaps the signs above the shop windows and window displays are illuminated at night. If there are pubs in your street, they might feature signs promising 'real ale' or 'pub food' in homely lettering. Now compare this with how your church looks from the outside. Are you using your noticeboard as well as other organisations in your street?

Look again at some of the posters in shop windows. Not only is the text in colour and accompanied by a photo, but it is likely to be large enough to be seen from the other side of the road. Could the same be said for the text on your existing noticeboard? One mistake often made is to try to fit too much information on – details of different kinds of services, contact details, times at which the parish office is open, and so on. It's usually too much for people to take in. If you reduce the amount of information, you can make the remaining text larger.

Think too about the style of typeface used. Many churches use a deliberately old-fashioned font, even if their services are lively, family-oriented ones using contemporary worship songs. Old-fashioned fonts suggest a reliable, conservative and established style that might be at odds with the reality. If that's the case, think carefully about using a more modern font. Generally speaking, sans serif fonts look more modern, while serif fonts look more traditional. Some fonts may not be appropriate, simply because the individual letters will be too thin to be seen from a distance. In general, it might be good to concentrate on 'bold' or 'black' versions of typefaces that you like.

Think too about colours. Many shops and businesses use

white text on a dark blue background (or white on purple, or yellow/gold on dark blue/purple), as these colours are most likely to catch someone's eye. Blue is also a colour that signals reliability and trustworthiness, so is perhaps appropriate for a church. Emblazoning your noticeboard with a kaleidoscope of different colours is not so appropriate unless you want your church to seem self-consciously 'wacky'.

If you decide to tear down your noticeboard and start again, you might also want to think about what it's made of. Sub-consciously, this affects what people think of your church. A wooden board looks more traditional, especially if painted with text in a serif typeface. An aluminium sign looks more modern, especially if it displays a logo and more avant garde lettering.

And if you're replacing the noticeboard, do think about adding your church's logo onto it in a prominent position. That way, when something drops through people's letter-boxes with your church's logo on, they should – consciously or sub-consciously – be able to associate it with the building they regularly pass.

How to do it:

1. Look at your existing noticeboard(s). What do the style of board, typefaces, size of lettering and colours say about your church? Would it benefit from a revamp?
2. Think about the kind of identity that your church wants to promote. If you are a young, vibrant congregation, is it time you replaced that wooden noticeboard with something more modern? What about the typeface used?

3. Re-design the text and the layout of your noticeboard, removing superfluous words so you can make the remaining text as large as possible. Add your church's logo.

4. Ask your signwriter to paint or produce your noticeboard in the appropriate colours for it to be easily noticed.

5. If you are creating more than one noticeboard, try to do them in a similar style.

29. Remove confusing references to 'First/Second/Third/Fourth Sundays', or to types of service.

Many churches hold different types of service at different times of the day on different Sundays of the month. No doubt church members become expert at remembering whether we have reached the third or fourth Sunday this month, and whether that means traditional Communion or family service. But for non-regulars, this can be another unnecessary hurdle to clear before they can actually attend. It might be more helpful to simplify those references to different types of service on different days.

If you are a non-regular churchgoer who passes a church every day, and the noticeboard simply says: '11am: Morning Worship', you might remember that. If there's a long list of different types of worship on different days, you might not absorb that as easily. For the more discerning churchgoer, you can, of course, include a more comprehensive list of what service happens when in your porch, or inside the church itself. But removing those details from your main external noticeboard means you can reduce the amount of text on it, and therefore make that text much larger.

Of course, you may particularly want to communicate that your church offers certain styles of worship. If you've decided to appeal to young families, you might want to indicate that certain services are 'family-friendly' in some way (either all-age worship or Sunday school is provided). If your church is aiming to become a place where high-quality music is always provided, you might want to indicate that too. But there are simple ways to do so, by using symbols next to the relevant services. This also means you can make both text and symbols larger on the noticeboard and hence easier to read. Examples can be found at www.getyourchurchnoticed.com.

How to do it:

1. Examine your noticeboard, if necessary with someone who doesn't regularly come to church. How confusing is your list of Sunday services?
2. Think about all-embracing names to describe your usual worship pattern – 10.30am could be Family Worship, Morning Worship or Celebration; 6.30pm could be Evening Worship, Informal Worship or Traditional Service, for instance. Replace your list of services on different Sundays of the month with your all-embracing phrase.
3. Think about appropriate symbols that you could use to denote information about types of service. A symbol showing a musical note can denote which services are sung. A stick figure of an adult holding a child's hand might show that a service is family-friendly.

30. Include a glass-fronted section to display posters.

You may already have compared your noticeboards to advertising billboards and shop window displays. Now think about how often you actually look at such displays as you walk or drive down your main street. The chances are that you look mostly when such displays change. Now think about how often your own noticeboard changes. If it's not very often, then it's possible that passers-by rarely look at it.

Inevitably, some information on your noticeboard won't change very often: the name of the church, times of services and name of the minister. But other information does change quite frequently: the dates and times of your latest 'big event', for instance (as decided by your communications team). So it makes sense to incorporate a section in at least one of your external noticeboards that can be used to publicise such events and activities. The best way is probably some kind of glass- or perspex-fronted section into which posters can be placed.

Advice about such posters will be examined in Ideas 55–56, but suffice it to say that the various guidelines on typeface, colour and size still apply. The person walking past on the opposite pavement or driving past in a car should still be able to read what it says.

Using posters to advertise your special events helps to reinforce details that may already have appeared in your parish magazine, on your website and in leaflets posted through letterboxes. It's important to remember that this is purely a reinforcement – few people will take the trouble to write down what's on the noticeboard. But it helps for them to see the same details in several different places or pieces of literature.

Some churches like to use posters that aim to promote churchgoing or the Gospel itself rather than special events. However, these posters are often inappropriate. It might be a picture of a beautiful view with a Bible verse printed in one corner, some kind of jokey reference (the classic is: 'What's missing from this Ch—rch? UR'), or a hand-painted slogan extolling the virtues of a Christian life. We live in a more sophisticated, media-savvy society than the one in which such slogans were invented. Compared with the billboard that features a beautifully photographed model and a witty one-liner, these posters simply seem out-dated, or seem to confirm that church-goers have a poor sense of humour. In any case, your communications team should have a list of events and activities they want to publicise on your noticeboard, so such posters should never be needed.

How to do it:

1. You may need to create a new noticeboard featuring a glass-fronted section, or revamp your existing one. It might be tempting to create a separate, stand-alone board purely for posters, but it is likely to be less effective than incorporating it into your main external noticeboard.
2. Consult with your communications team about events and activities to publicise. Draw up a timetable for changing the posters regularly.
3. Recruit someone who will do this job. It might be appropriate to have the same person changing them on both the external noticeboard and the ones inside church to

ensure a seamless changeover from publicity of one event to the next.

4. Consult Ideas 55–56 to discover how best to create posters.

31. Include up-to-date contact details for ministers and others.

Churches are often good at including contact details of ministers and other church leaders on their external noticeboards. Imagine the difference it might make to the service at your local supermarket if the manager's home phone number was displayed prominently outside!

It's important that those details are correct. Sometimes contact details are updated in a way that looks temporary: a small piece of wood with the new minister's name on may be glued over the old name, as if their tenure is likely to be limited. While it is undoubtedly very 'customer-friendly' to include the minister's name on the external noticeboard, if you are revamping your board just at the wrong time, it might go out of date within months. Think about whether it might be better to put the word 'Minister' (or 'Vicar' or 'Pastor') and a general office phone number, plus perhaps also 'Parish office' and a number, 'Youth minister' and a number and so on. That way, your noticeboard could remain free of 'corrections' for a few years!

Of course, there may be a point at which some corrections are necessary. It's always helpful to go back to the person who created your original sign, if possible. Amateur attempts to paint over a name or the time of a service with an update will usually look amateur. The original manufacturer or painter is likely to make a better job.

How to do it:

1. Check that the contact details of your minister are correct.
2. If you can, make the necessary changes as you revamp the noticeboard. If you are in any doubt about whether someone might still be in the same job in a year's time, don't include their name, just their position.
3. Include phone numbers, not addresses (too much text) or e-mail addresses (they are likely to change too frequently).

32. Put your website address on your noticeboard.

Many churches have a website with reams of information about their history, activities and events, but don't put the address on their external noticeboard. This seems peculiar, especially when you look at how keen other organisations are to publicise web addresses. With more and more people having access to the web, this is a significant item that shouldn't be overlooked.

One advantage of putting your website address on the noticeboard is that the website is a convenient place to put all sorts of information for non-regulars, including the times and styles of services, how to make enquiries about baptisms, weddings and funerals and what kind of weekly activities go on. It means that you *don't* need to put this information on your noticeboard, as some churches are tempted to do.

Including a website address on a church noticeboard in itself makes your church look more cutting-edge, regardless of what's actually on your website! Passers-by won't necessarily commit the address to memory. But if they remember you are on the web, they may search for it via a search engine. If they hadn't seen your website address, they may not have thought to do so.

How to do it:

1. Obviously, it's important to have a website or create one first. See Ideas 79–85 for more details on this.
2. If you are revamping your noticeboard anyway, it should be easy to include your website address on it. If not, see if you can find a space at the bottom to include it.

33. Use an electronic moving display board.

Sometimes it's good to look at how other institutions or organisations communicate and appropriate their methods. Partly that's because people are more likely to look at what you're saying if you're communicating in a way they don't expect. Seeing a traditional poster on a church noticeboard might not rate a second glance, but seeing the vicar abseil down the church tower holding a banner certainly would.

One idea is to use electronic (LED) display boards to convey information about your services and activities. These can be single-line displays, perhaps with the words scrolling across, or multi-line displays such as those used at cinemas, leisure centres or railway stations. This may only be appropriate for certain styles of church – probably the less formal house or community churches. But it does allow you to convey a lot of information in an easy way, and a way that is likely to catch the eye of passers-by.

Larger churches may even use video display boards that enable them to display text, photos and video of church activities to passers-by. This kind of video board is regularly used at railway stations, conference centres and in the foyers of large firms. Remember that if this is being shown externally, you'll only be able to show pictures, not sound.

How to do it:

1. Investigate how much an LED display board might cost.
2. Talk to your church's leadership about the effectiveness of such a display board, given the location of your church. Do enough people actually walk past your building to make the expenditure worthwhile?
3. Decide how you will programme the board, and then keep it updated. Is it something that could be done by your parish office? As with many other things, it's important to make sure the display changes over time to reflect forthcoming events and priorities.

Community Needs

34. Survey the physical and social needs of your community – and use your building to meet some of them.

As Christians, we are called to help transform our communities. It's not just a matter of saving souls: it's also about standing against injustice, looking after the marginalised and helping to spread God's values through service and sacrifice.

Churches are good at helping to meet people's needs through lunch clubs, coffee mornings or parent and toddler groups. But often these ideas come because church leaders or congregation members think they are good ideas (or someone felt there was a need 20 years ago, and your church activities haven't changed since!). Sometimes, the result can be a handful of people turning up for a coffee morning that might be of little interest to the vast majority of local residents. Yet your church building may be the only large meeting place in the entire neighbourhood. Might there be a way of using it more effectively?

How often does a church actually ask what the wider community would like *before* organising its activities? How often do we audit the socio-economic make-up of our community, using some of the local authority or census data that is freely available? Perhaps there is a desperate need for a youth club, after-school club or meeting place for the recently bereaved in your area, and your church would be the ideal location for it – but it hasn't happened because no one has thought of it. A survey may tell you some of these things.

Such surveys of local needs were the basis of the 'Kairos' process run by the Anglican Diocese of Portsmouth in 2004–05. Fascinating facts about the physical, social and spiritual needs of the community were thrown up. Parishes responded by organising activities that would help to meet those needs. In some cases, that involved modernising or revamping their buildings to create new community facilities.

The benefits of such an approach should be obvious. The reputation of your church as a place where people are ready to serve the needs of others is enhanced; your congregation gets the chance to meet more people from their local community; and more unchurched people actually pass through your church building, meaning they may be less intimidated by crossing the threshold for worship too.

How to do it:

1. Devise a survey that includes open-ended questions such as 'What do you think are the biggest problems in this area?', 'In which areas does your family need help?' or 'What could [insert name of your church] do to help?'
2. You could conduct your survey by calling on people's

homes or standing in shopping centres, though people are often suspicious of such methods. See if you can find more consumer-friendly ways of approaching people: perhaps by sending survey forms through the post, or within a local authority's mailing. Include stamped addressed envelopes, or find a convenient place for them to drop off completed forms.

3. If your questions have been genuinely open-ended, it will take you some time to analyse the survey results. Spend as much time as it takes, so you can be sure of getting it right. Do they suggest one area of over-riding concern?

4. Visit your local authority or library to discover census results and socio-economic indicators for your local area, or find them on the internet. Again, spend time analysing those results. Is one particular group (asylum seekers, students, children under five or the over-80s) over-represented in your area?

5. Consider what secular authorities, government agencies, voluntary groups and churches of other denominations already do for these types of people or to help tackle the issues you have discovered. It may be helpful not to replicate what they do, or alternatively to work in partnership with them to help reach a wider group of people (see Idea 35).

6. Consider whether improvements or changes to your church building may be needed to make it suitable for community use.

7. Decide what activities you should start doing to help meet some of those needs. Publicise this in your congregation and in the media, emphasising that you are responding to identified needs.

8. Decide what activities you may want to *stop* doing because those needs may simply not be as great in your neighbourhood, or because you have identified higher priorities.

Further resources:

For more information about the 'Kairos' process in Portsmouth's Anglican diocese, see: www.portsmouth. anglican.org

35. Liaise with your local authority to discover which local needs are not being met, and work with them to try to meet them.

In many areas, churches are trying to tackle similar issues to the secular authorities – but in a different way. If there are lots of teenagers in a particular neighbourhood, you may find both a local authority-run youth club, and a church-run club. The former may be staffed with professionals and may have a budget for resources. The church-run club may be staffed with well-meaning volunteers and have little money, and may also be trying to meet the spiritual needs of the teenagers. In some places, both types of club may be necessary. In other areas, secular and church authorities may find they are doing similar things – perhaps even with the same teenagers or on the same night of each week.

Local authorities and the UK government used to be suspicious of faith-based initiatives. Funding was not often given to activities run by churches, meaning that congregations grew used to funding and staffing their own. These days, there is more chance of being able to work in partnership. The government may discover that its target of reducing youth crime, for instance, can be met more easily by funding a church-run youth club that already exists. That shouldn't mean that the church becomes an arm of the government and stops having a spiritual input into teenagers' lives. But it may affect how the church chooses to outline the purposes of its youth club, especially in any bid for funding.

And what happens when your church becomes a trusted provider of local services? Its reputation is enhanced – not just by those on the receiving end, but also by those professionals working in national and local government. Your church's efforts may be seen as they really are: a genuine attempt to make a difference to society, rather than a scarcely veiled cover for winning converts. This is the kind of thing that wins admiration for the Church's role rather than breeds cynicism about it.

How to do it:

1. Talk to your local authority about what it is doing in specific areas, such as work with young people, care for the elderly, projects for the homeless or asylum seekers.
2. Compare what the local authority is doing with what your church is doing already in this area. Could you work in partnership together, or are two different approaches needed?
3. Look at your church building. Is there a way in which you could re-develop it to help meet some of those needs?

4. Keep an eye out for national government initiatives that appear to be replicating what your church is already doing. Could you bid for funding so that your church becomes a trusted provider of those services?
5. Many professionals these days will have experience of 'bidding' for funding. Learn from their experiences so that your church knows how to express its concerns in the right way in application forms.

Further resources:

See *Faithworks: Unpacked* by Steve Chalke on how to get funding for your project or visit www.faithworks.info

36. Meet spiritual needs outside Sunday services.

There is no rule that says that acts of communal worship have to take place on a Sunday. Yet we concentrate so much on filling our pews for a Sunday service that we often miss the chances to engage with people's spirituality in the rest of the week. Sunday morning may be a bad time for many – the party on the Saturday night, the weekend visits to relatives, the commitment to DIY or sport, or the weekend job may all get in the way. Rather than bemoaning this state of affairs, it might be better to think of the bigger picture.

Providing spiritual input during activities in the rest of the week may actually prove more effective. If you already bring together a group of parents on a weekday morning with their young children, why not create a ten-minute toddler-friendly service for them all to attend afterwards? If you are a city centre church, why not create a brief act of worship that business people can attend in their lunch hour? None of this has to be particularly formal – it might be a hymn or song, a brief thought and a prayer. For some of these people, who might never dream of coming on a Sunday, that might be 'church' for them.

For those who work in chaplaincy in schools, universities, prisons, hospitals or other institutions, the non-Sunday style of worship will be very familiar. For the vast majority of the time, the ministry of those chaplains may be limited to brief prayers by the bedside or words of comfort in the cell. That doesn't make it any less important. In fact, it could be argued that these ministries are actually *more* important, because these chaplains are coming alongside people where they already are, rather than expecting them to have to cross the threshold of a church.

How to do it:

1. Look at the midweek activities that your church hosts. Consider if there is a way of creating some kind of spiritual input into those activities, if there isn't one already.
2. Look at the location of your church. Are there opportunities to attract local residents or those who work in the area to short midweek acts of worship?
3. What kind of 'chaplaincy'-type activities could your church take on? Is there a shopping centre nearby where the managers would appreciate someone who could support and minister to retailers? Is there a large employer that might like a chaplain to be available for employees to talk to? Remember that a 'chaplain' needn't necessarily be an ordained minister.

37. Create an after-school or holiday club for children.

For many non-churchgoers, memories of Sunday school or coming to church as a child are important factors in choosing to attend church later in life. A bad experience can turn someone off faith completely. Good experiences can create a latent sense of faith, which subsequent events can reawaken.

But fewer children come to children's groups on Sundays. If parents find it increasingly difficult to get to church, so will their children. While family life at the weekend may be busier, the increase in the number of families where both parents work may create a different opportunity. Many families are looking for somewhere reliable to send their children between the end of the school day and the end of the working day. After-school clubs run by churches – with fun activities and spiritual input – may be one way of plugging the gap left by the decline in children's attendance on Sundays. The same applies to school holidays, when both parents may still be working or busy in other ways. They may appreciate the chance to drop off children at holiday clubs for a morning or a whole day.

Again, the advantage of this approach is that the church becomes a trusted provider of services within the community, enhancing its reputation. The interface with parents as they drop off or pick up their children is a valuable chance for church and unchurched people to mix.

Another opportunity has presented itself in the UK. Since 2005, the government's Extended Schools Initiative has meant schools are open from 8am to 6pm, offering activities such as homework clubs, sport, music tuition, clubs, visits and even business activities. Churches can offer to run some of those activities in partnership with local schools, or even to host some of those activities.

How to do it:

1. Find out about the current provision of after-school or holiday care from your local education authority. What facilities exist in your area?
2. Discover if there is any national or local funding for such an initiative, or if you can work in partnership with your local school.
3. Decide where to hold an after-school or holiday club. Your church building may or may not be the best place.
4. Recruit a paid, qualified professional to run it, as well as volunteer helpers. They should be able to put together a comprehensive programme of spiritual and other activities. Ensure all volunteers are put through child protection procedures.
5. Publicise the after-school club or holiday club with leaflets and posters. Liaise with your local school or uniformed organisations so that such leaflets can be handed out to children and parents.
6. Take details of the children who attend and follow up the initial contact with visits to their homes or invitations to other events.

Further resources:

For more information about the UK government's Extended Schools Initiative, see: www.dfes.gov.uk

38. Invite professionals who work in your community to meet congregation members and ask how local Christians can help them in their jobs.

In any given community, there are probably a large number of professionals – MPs, teachers, social workers, police, health workers and many others – who aim to help people. The local church also exists to care for those within its community. It's surprising that so few churches have tried to bring together all those who work in the same locality to compare notes. The Church also has a spiritual function, but in many other respects it might be trying to do a similar kind of job.

Many working in these areas may appreciate getting together to discover common strands in their jobs. They may realise that others are supporting the same families or dealing with the same issues, but from a different perspective. And the local minister is often a good, 'neutral' person to chair such a meeting, in that he or she should have no particular departmental or party political axe to grind. Such a forum may discover issues such as crippling personal debt or high levels of family breakdown that can be addressed by the creation of a credit union or some teaching on parenting skills. The chances are that each professional organisation or agency involved wouldn't have been able to tackle that problem alone.

This is why the UK government now requires each local authority area to set up Local Strategic Partnerships, made up of those from the public, private, community and voluntary sectors. They aim to tackle deep-seated, multi-faceted problems that require responses from many different bodies. Its members draw up a Community Strategy in consultation with the local community. Often a representative of faith communities will serve on such a body already. Clearly, if this organisation already exists, it makes no sense for the local church to replicate it.

But if local Christians tell their Local Strategic Partnership or community forum that they are happy to help the disadvantaged in appropriate ways, it provides an excellent example of community service. Once again, the local church becomes a trusted provider of services, and hopefully a catalyst for social change, adding to its reputation in the area.

How to do it:

1. If some kind of community forum or Local Strategic Partnership already exists in your area, check its membership and future priorities. If appropriate, offer the services of Christians at your church to help with implementing some of those priorities.
2. If such a forum doesn't exist, list the agencies working in your neighbourhood in healthcare, education, social services, youth work, crime prevention and community regeneration. Write to them, as well as local politicians. Ask if they would like help in their jobs from local Christians, and invite them to meet to discuss it.
3. Meet with representatives from those agencies. Act on suggestions given to you by these professionals.
4. Work towards creating some kind of forum where these issues can be discussed by all the agencies together. Offer to chair it, if necessary.

5. Find creative ways in which this forum could help to meet the needs of the community – perhaps by lobbying local or national government on the community's behalf, or finding joint solutions that would not have been possible for each of the agencies individually.
6. Stop meeting if you feel your work is done. Such a forum should not necessarily become a permanent feature.

Further resources:

The Faithworks Movement, set up by the Revd Steve Chalke, has done much pioneering work in the area of helping to meet community needs. See www.faithworks. info for details. The charity Credit Action helps Christians to help others to avoid the crippling burden of debt. See www.creditaction.com for details.

Welcome Pack

39. Produce a welcome pack with essential information about church activities.

Imagine someone new has started coming to church services, or to one of your church activities. How might they discover more about what else happens at your church? Would they need to wait for an announcement to discover that there is a regular keep-fit club there? Would it be up to fellow congregation members to tell them about Bible study groups? Or would they need to scour the church for leaflets or posters about the range of activities?

One way to make it easier for newcomers is to put together a comprehensive guide to church activities in a handy welcome pack. It can tell them about styles of worship at different Sunday services, midweek activities, church groups and give full contact details. It might encourage fringe or newer members of your church to get involved in other activities that bring them into contact with more and more Christians. These days, when 'belonging' to a church often comes before 'believing', this can only be a good thing.

There are a variety of ways to do this, but the principle

should be that individual items within the pack should be easy to update. If you produce one coherent brochure advertising all church activities, it only takes one phone number or e-mail address to change to make it out of date. It's easier to update a pack that has a professionally printed cover, into which you insert a series of different leaflets, each publicising a different aspect of church life. As circumstances change, each leaflet can be updated and replaced in the remaining packs.

You might want to include a card within the pack that people can fill in, post to the church office or hand to the minister as they leave. This might be a request for a pastoral visit, an application to join an Alpha course or simply a request to be kept in touch with church activities.

This could easily be done on an ecumenical basis, which might make the initial outlay on printing costs more affordable and would also help to communicate the unity between denominations in your area. Your map could show the location of all churches in the locality. It might sound natural to suggest that each leaflet inside the pack should refer to activities in one church. But another way of doing it might be to group together all family activities on one leaflet, activities for the elderly on another, youth activities on a third, and so on. This will help to cement the fact that these activities actually complement each other, rather than being run by competing churches.

How to do it:

1. Approach other churches in your locality to see if they would be interested in producing an ecumenical welcome pack.

2. Examine what leaflets you produce at the moment publicising different aspects of church life. Are they produced in a similar, consistent way, or in different ways by the different groups concerned?

3. If you are happy with the range of information you already produce, you may only need to think about producing a cover. This might be an A4 or A5 'wallet', into which your leaflets are inserted. Examine whether this might be professionally printed. It could be in colour, and include photos of churchgoers on the front and a map showing the location of your churches, church halls and other relevant buildings on the back. As you design this, do make sure you only include details of things that are unlikely to change (i.e. the address and location of church buildings), rather than names and contact details that may change over time.

4. You might want to get 500 or so of the 'wallets' printed to start with to keep you going for a while.

5. If you need to update your leaflets, or create some new ones publicising aspects of church life for the first time, create a consistent 'look' to the leaflets, using the same fonts and your church/ecumenical logo. Information about different activities could be photocopied onto different coloured pieces of paper.

6. One way of making the pack easy to use is to fold the pieces of paper so that the headings for each leaflet can be seen when the pack is first opened.

40. Leave welcome packs in public places and give them to those who enquire about baptisms, weddings and funerals.

Once you have a welcome pack that you are happy with, you might want to make it available in public places such as libraries, GPs' surgeries, tourist information centres and council offices. People can then access the information without necessarily coming to your church building. This is where it will pay for your pack to look as professional as possible – a few photocopied leaflets by themselves might be overlooked, whereas a pack with a glossy, colour cover may be picked up.

Obviously, you will have to ask permission from the surgery, local authority or library in question to display your literature there. Sometimes those kinds of places are reluctant to display information of a religious nature. It might be worth pointing out that your activities are open to all, regardless of faith. And if you are working in partnership with your local authority to provide an after-school club, it would seem churlish for them not to allow you to publicise its existence.

How to do it:

1. Approach various public bodies and ask their permission to display your welcome packs. Give each location a handful.
2. Monitor regularly how many welcome packs are taken – or whether over-zealous officials have removed them completely.
3. As the information is updated, provide replacement welcome packs for each location and take away old ones to be updated.

41. Ask congregation members to give packs to new neighbours as they move into their street.

Another way to get your welcome packs into the hands of people who move into your neighbourhood is to use your congregation members. They should be able to spot when someone new moves into their road, and can introduce themselves and hand over a pack. Most of us have experienced the trauma of moving house and finding ourselves in a new place with no friends. Most of us would appreciate having someone call on us in those initial few days. And the personal contact could lead to a neighbourly friendship, whether the family concerned comes to church or not.

Having a welcome pack may be a good excuse for people to pop in on new neighbours – or perhaps to renew acquaintances with existing neighbours. If a family have children, churchgoers can hand a pack over suggesting they may be interested in the after-school club or mothers and toddlers group. Because congregation members are not directly inviting people to come to church services, this can be a very non-threatening form of evangelism.

What might make your church's welcome pack particularly attractive to such people is a map and some contact details for other local amenities – GPs' surgeries, chemists, the post office, banks and so on. If you include such details, you're not only helping newcomers discover where those amenities are, you're also increasing the chances that they will hang on to your welcome pack.

How to do it:

1. Produce a map and contact details for local amenities. Include that sheet in those packs given to people who have moved into the area.
2. Discover where your congregation members live. Get a map of the area, and ask people to stick pins into it to represent their homes. If you have two or more people on the same street, they might want to divide it between them.
3. Provide each member of the congregation with half a dozen or so welcome packs. Invite them to give them to existing neighbours to start with.
4. Suggest that congregation members could look out for houses that are 'For Sale', then 'Sold'. When they spot the new people moving in, they can pop round with a welcome pack and a word of welcome.

5. In some cases, an enterprising church member might want to host a 'getting to know you' evening for existing or new neighbours, perhaps over a meal. Welcome packs might also be available there.

42. Include a DVD or video showing church activities within your welcome pack.

We've already established that still photos are more appealing than text-based literature. Moving images are even better. So, if you have the technology and the expertise in the church – or you can afford to pay someone who has – then producing a DVD or video of church activities will certainly help to get it noticed.

It's a way of non-churchgoers being able to get a feel for what your church does from the comfort of their own living room. It helps them to appreciate the breadth of what you can offer without having to cross your threshold. We can underestimate the impact it can have on non-regulars to see people enjoying worship, fellowship and church activities.

It might sound prohibitively expensive to pay for someone to produce a professional video or DVD, or to pay for a member of your congregation to get the relevant equipment. But it might be instructive to add up how much your church spends on written items of church literature, most of which may be churned out with little regard for cost of paper, ink, photocopying and so on. When you compare the costs – and take into account that a video or DVD could be ten times as effective as a written brochure – it may well represent decent value for money.

How to do it:

1. Check whether any member of your congregation has the necessary equipment to produce a video or DVD – camcorder, digital editing equipment and the relevant software to produce digital videos or DVDs.

2. If not, there may be someone who has a camcorder for personal use. Ask whether they would be prepared to take on this role.

3. Provide the relevant equipment and training. Your volunteer may need to enrol on a college course in order to understand how to edit and produce videos or DVDs. The college tutor should also be able to give advice on what equipment to buy.

4. If that isn't possible, investigate the possibility of hiring a freelancer to record, edit and produce a video or DVD for you.

5. Make a list of which church activities you would like to feature. Perhaps you might also produce a draft script for your volunteer or professional video person to follow.

6. Approach those involved in activities around the church and discover when would be the best times to film them in action – perhaps if they are having a special outing, one-off activity or if there is a significant church service. Create a filming timetable.

7. Find someone who is prepared to 'front' the film, as a presenter or narrator. They may be filmed in the various settings, or their narration added as a voiceover.

8. Give your volunteer or professional enough time to edit and produce the videos or DVDs. Decide how you would like to use them: will you put one in every welcome

pack, or only give them to those who have a direct link with the church, such as wedding couples, those with children who are getting baptised, or those who are interested in enrolling on Alpha courses?

Internal Displays

43. Re-organise the location of internal display boards.

Walk into a typical church and you'll probably find a wealth of information all around you on various display boards about special services, church activities, community events and more. But those internal display boards are often located in a seemingly random way. Little thought may have been given to precisely where they are placed within the building. Is there any point in publicising events in the church porch, which is so small that no one actually lingers there long enough to read anything? Or what about those display boards at the back of your worship area? Do church-goers ever stare at the notices on the back wall on a normal Sunday morning?

When considering where to put internal displays, do think of which audience you are trying to reach. For instance, if your church building is often locked, but the porch is open all day, it makes sense to put posters advertising outreach events there, as well as contact details for clergy, a detailed diary of service times, and perhaps a phone number for the Samaritans – many desperate people think about finding refuge in church buildings. If your church hall is constantly being used by different community groups, display boards in the hall will be valuable for communicating information about special events. But if your church building itself is open for tourists, your main displays would be more use there. And if you have created an attractive 'foyer' area for visitors to look around, that will be the prime location for them.

If you are particularly trying to reach members of your congregation with important information, how should you do it? You could put your display boards wherever they have coffee after the service, rather than in the worship area. And we've already seen that we usually notice things only when they change, so why not change the location of your displays regularly? That might mean buying a portable display board that can be wheeled into several different places. If something is really important for your congregation to see, why not place it just inside the entrance to your church, so worshippers literally have to walk around it?

There are other ways to impress the importance of a particular event on your congregation, of course, and combining them can be very effective. A high-profile display combined with a verbal notice and leaflets given out to each member of the congregation would make it hard to miss. One church advertised its 'vision day', which happened to be on Valentine's Day, by filling heart-shaped, red balloons with helium and attaching them to the end of each pew. Each had 'Vision Day: February 14' written on it. Delighted children took them home, meaning each family had a reminder about it in their home.

How to do it:

1. Think about the location of the display boards around your church in relation to the 'audience' you want to reach with each. Are they in prime locations for tourists and visitors or for regular churchgoers to see?
2. Remove superfluous displays and noticeboards, and any that are starting to show their age. Sub-consciously, people will think notices on a tatty noticeboard are less important.
3. If necessary, invest in new noticeboards and display boards. Portable ones will give you the greatest flexibility.
4. Move your portable display boards around so they are in the best location for each activity that takes place in your church. If they are in church during the service, wheel them into the place where people have coffee afterwards.

44. Re-organise the content of your display boards to help people access information more easily.

Once you've got the location of your display boards sorted out, turn your attention to what is actually displayed. Perhaps different items are added by different people, seemingly at random or in any available space. And no one removes the out-of-date, tatty and dog-eared posters. No wonder people get confused.

Your posters and notices will probably fall into several distinct categories – 'Church Events', 'Community Events', 'Overseas Mission', 'Children and Young People' and so on.

Simply by creating these headings for each of your displays, you can bring a semblance of organisation to them. You can divide one display board into several sections, each with a different heading, or, if you have enough, you can have a different board for each category. People will be able to tell at a glance where to look for the information they need.

Then there are the priorities set by your communications team. If it has identified 'world mission' as the priority for the next six months, make sure you earmark the display board in the best location for this issue. That doesn't necessarily mean that it will remain unchanged for those six months – there might be a series of different displays on the same topic; or you might temporarily advertise your summer fair on that board before returning to the mission theme afterwards.

Once you've thrown away the dog-eared, out-of-date and faded posters, and are happy with the location and content of your displays, you'll want to make sure it stays that way. Why not identify someone to be in charge of your

display boards? This person might be someone who is regularly in your building anyway – a caretaker, church-warden or office administrator – and so can check when posters go out of date or need replacing. Congregation members should be told to give posters to this person, rather than try to pin them up themselves. That way, the displays remain organised and up to date. And if the person is also part of the communications team, they will know your priorities.

The same, of course, applies to leaflets, brochures, newsletters and many other things that might be displayed on tables rather than pinned to boards. Many of these items might have been sent to your church office or placed there by congregation members, without necessarily any thought as to whether they are of interest to the wider congregation. If your poster co-ordinator is given responsibility for check-ing these items too, those that are out of date or less of a priority can be removed, giving a higher profile to items that you want people to pick up and keep.

How to do it:

1. Look at the posters and leaflets currently displayed or available in your church. Could they be re-organised, using headings to distinguish different types of informa-tion?
2. Consider how you might create displays of the issues identified as the most important by the communications team. Which display board is in the prime location for this? Could such displays be regularly changed, even if they focus on the same issue?

3. Recruit a 'poster co-ordinator' to be in charge of displays, posters, noticeboards and literature available for people to take away.
4. Make sure the congregation know who your poster co-ordinator is and make it clear that all literature to be displayed should be given to them.

45. Create a display of photos or a video showing people involved in church activities.

Once people are inside your church building, what's the best way of showing them the range of activities that your congregation gets up to? Covering a noticeboard with lots of text-based information? Giving them leaflets to take away? These things have their place, but it's the visual that is likely to appeal most. A display of photos of church members involved in one-off activities like outings and dinners, or regular activities such as lunches and children's groups, will elicit interest. It should also give an idea of the size and age range of your congregation.

Taking good photos these days is fairly easy, especially with digital technology. Beware, though, as digital photos that look good on screen may not look so good when printed out, unless you have the right kind of photographic paper and a high resolution picture. It can be more effective to take non-digital photos and have them developed professionally. Whichever method you use, the resultant photos can be arranged at random, or can be separated into different kinds of activity. It's tempting to take lots of photos of children and young people, especially if you want to emphasise the youthfulness of your congregation. Be careful,

though, as you'll need to get permission from the parents of the children involved before displaying them.

If you have the technology, it might be good to put such photos on some kind of PowerPoint display, which will project lots of different images onto a wall or screen. The advantage of this is that you can mix text with photos, giving brief explanations of each activity. And if you have a camcorder, you can even create a video showing church activities that can be displayed in the same way. Moving images are even more effective at conveying what happens in your church. You may need to make sure such technology is either securely attached to your walls, capable of being locked away or removed from church when there is no one there, for security reasons.

How to do it:

1. Recruit someone to take photos at various one-off events and regular activities run by your church. This might be the same person who covers such events for your church magazine or newsletter (see Idea 65).
2. Display the photos on a display board. Make sure it is situated near the entrance to the church, so that visitors and newcomers can easily see it.
3. You can label groups of photos with the name of the group or activity, but it shouldn't be necessary to give a caption to each one.
4. If you can create a PowerPoint display of still images or a video, set it up in the same kind of location.
5. Review the content of the display board and/or presentation at regular intervals, adding new photos or images as appropriate.

46. Create a display of children's work or a children's corner, to show that the church is genuinely family-friendly.

One thing that eagled-eyed parents may look for when visiting your church for the first time is evidence that your services are family-friendly. There are various ways to do this (not least by publicising your family or all-age services), but one way to show the importance you place on your children and young people is to give them space for their own displays.

This could be a special display board that you allow the Sunday school or youth group to use exclusively. Giving them this kind of responsibility will also help them to feel valued in the church community. Younger children will be proud to see their work displayed. Teenagers will want to highlight an issue that is important to them. In either case, those displays will communicate your commitment to younger people even if none are actually in church when people visit.

Another way to do so is to create a children's corner at the back of church, including books, toys, child-sized tables and chairs. This will serve a practical purpose during church services: parents can keep their children occupied there if the service itself is not family-friendly or if their children are too young for Sunday school groups. The temptation might be to clear this equipment away during the week, but leaving it out suggests to visitors that your church thinks children are important. An alternative is to provide toys that don't make a noise for children to play with during services. They could be placed in cloth bags and hung at the end of each pew. These too will communicate your family-friendly credentials.

How to do it:

1. Ask the leaders of your children's groups and youth group if they would like to have a dedicated noticeboard for displays.
2. If they do, identify which one(s) they can have and give

them the responsibility for filling it. This might involve some initial encouragement about the kind of thing that might be appropriate.

3. Encourage them to keep changing the display(s) at regular intervals.

4. If you have a children's corner in your church, consider whether it is possible to leave the equipment out during the week.

5. Invite congregation members to contribute suitable toys to place in cloth bags at the ends of your pews, or that can be given to families as they enter.

Church Services

47. Recruit a welcome team of people who can talk to newcomers or visitors as they arrive.

For many non-churchgoers, coming to church is an intimidating experience. They may not know anyone else who goes, or what to wear. They may worry about not knowing the right jargon, the words to the hymns, when to stand up and sit down, or even whether people will be judgemental about their lifestyle. For those of us who go to church, it's easy to forget how it feels to cross the threshold for the first time. The nearest equivalent for us might be to visit a mosque – you may have a hazy idea of what goes on, but you would be terrified about causing offence by doing something inappropriate.

Imagine, then, if such people came to your church and not a single person spoke to them to help allay such fears. It does happen. The satirical Christian website Ship of Fools has been sending 'Mystery Worshippers' (Christians posing as first-time visitors) to investigate how welcoming churches are in the UK, US and Australia. The extent to which such mystery worshippers are welcomed is best described as patchy.

So it's a good idea to have a team of people who can welcome newcomers or visitors as they arrive for a church service. These people *could* be the same set of people as those who hand out books or leaflets, but it might be better to create an entirely different team. They might not only say hello, but show people to their seats, chat to them about why they have come and make sure they know about the location of crèche, Sunday school and toilets, and where coffee is served. Those people could also look out for newcomers looking lost after the service. While it's not typically British to approach people openly and introduce yourself, most newcomers do appreciate it.

Many churches already have welcome teams for newcomers, but something that's often overlooked is what happens if those people come back. It is, of course, the responsibility of the whole congregation – not just a particular team – to integrate people into the life of the church. In the most welcoming congregations, the newcomers would be introduced to different people each week, perhaps hearing more about various activities and selecting those they might like to join in. But often regulars are busy chatting to each other while the welcome team is busy welcoming brand new people.

How to do it:

1. Recruit a welcome team of people whose job it is to spot newcomers. You might like to recruit a few separate teams so they can be placed on a rota system.
2. Provide training for your welcome team about how to spot and approach newcomers in a suitable and not

overbearing way. Give them welcome packs or other church literature to give to newcomers explaining more about church activities.

3. Welcome team members may want to keep a special eye on families. Even if someone has told them about Sunday school at the start of the service, it might be good if someone helps the family to find out exactly where each child is going.

4. Encourage the rest of the congregation to help, not just with welcoming newcomers, but with continuing to make people feel welcome as they come to church on subsequent occasions.

Further resources:

To read Mystery Worshipper reports on the Ship of Fools website, see: www.ship-of-fools.com

48. Use PowerPoint technology to ensure a scrolling display of information and photos about church activities or forthcoming events.

In some churches, PowerPoint software is already used with laptops and data projectors to display liturgy, song words or sermon headings. If your church already has that technology, it should be relatively easy to use it to emphasise details of events or activities too. Such displays could include information about what's happening next Sunday, forthcoming events, or church activities that your communications team has identified as priorities. Using software such as PowerPoint means that you can use colour, include photos of those events or activities, or animate your text.

This can be used before the service starts, but some congregations may prefer to use that time for private prayer. If so, switching on the PowerPoint display while people are having coffee afterwards can also help to reinforce verbal notices already given, or information on weekly leaflets or posters.

How to do it:

1. If you already have PowerPoint technology, check who puts presentations together and operates the system. It may be that your parish office or magazine editor can supply that person with details of forthcoming events for them to display.
2. Decide when to use such displays. If you decide to do so after church services, and your coffee is not served in the worship area, you may need to move your technology into the room where coffee is served.
3. Ensure the presentation includes photos of activities or events as often as possible.
4. Ensure the presentation is changed regularly to reflect different priorities, and to include new events and recently taken photos.

49. Connect a video camera to the PowerPoint technology so people at the back of church can see what's happening at the front.

If you already possess a data projector to display PowerPoint presentations, it can also be used to project video images. This may be useful if you want to play videos during the worship service to emphasise a point. If yours is a large church, it can also be used with a video camera as a way of showing those sat at the back what is happening via a large screen. This can be especially useful during a family service, if children are called to the front of church to help with an activity. It is, of course, possible to combine several video cameras, a mixing desk and several screens around a very large church to transmit the whole service, but this may be beyond your congregation's resources. Using a church member's personal video camera together with the church's existing data projector and screen is an easier and cheaper way of doing it.

You can, of course, also use this technology to record what's happening elsewhere, for instance in children's groups, and play it shortly afterwards to the rest of the congregation. If yours is the kind of church where children are encouraged to report back to the congregation about what they have been doing in their Sunday school groups, a video camera can be an ideal way to do so.

How to do it:

1. Investigate whether one of your congregation members owns a video camera and is willing to use it in this way.
2. Ask the person concerned to connect their video camera to your data projector and film during services when you know it will be important for people at the back to see what is going on at the front.
3. In some churches, this may involve closing some curtains or covering some windows to avoid sunshine falling on the screen. Experiment to see if this is necessary.

4. Offer the technology to your children's groups in case they want to show what they do to the rest of the congregation at the end of the service.

50. Create a video montage of church activities and use it in church.

If you have the technology to show things happening 'live' in church services, you'll also have the ability to record events happening and allow other congregation members to watch them happening. You could record the church holiday or a church outing and play extracts during or after Sunday services. Or you could record a montage of church activities, perhaps based on those your communications team has decided are a priority. It makes a real difference for church members to see what actually goes on at the mother and toddler group or the midweek fellowship before they commit themselves to going, or tell friends about it. Such footage could also be used within church during the week, to give visitors and tourists an idea of what your church activities are like.

Digital video technology means that, with the right software, it's possible for the keen amateur camera operator to edit footage to the required length. Commissioning them to produce five minutes of footage about a particular group may require them to record at a couple of sessions, to create a script and find someone to narrate it, and then to edit the two together, but this is quite possible to do within a few weeks.

How to do it:

1. Discover if any of the video enthusiasts in your congregation could create a short film about particular church activities or outings.
2. Discover if they also have the software to edit images together to create a montage featuring one or more church activities.
3. Commission them to make a short video that can be used in services or midweek, using your existing PowerPoint technology.
4. Decide when might be an appropriate time to feature this video, perhaps within a church service when the leader is talking about what activities your church offers, or after a service while coffee is served.
5. If your enthusiast can produce several copies of a video or DVD featuring church activities, think about ways in which they can be distributed to those within your community.

51. Make greater use of the symbolic or the visual during sermons.

Video is, of course, just one visual format for presenting information. There are many others. Preachers are often good at using them during family services, where the use of drama, colourful props, visual aids and overhead projector slides is commonplace. As a result, many of us may remember what we've heard for several weeks afterwards. But we seem to think that adults don't need such visual stimuli, so most sermons are purely verbal. The result is that many are instantly forgettable.

It's a shame, as many other aspects of our services do use the symbolic and the visual. The breaking of the bread during Communion symbolises Jesus' body being broken for us; the immersion of believers during baptism marks the transition from spiritual death to life; and the washing of feet in Maundy Thursday services aptly describes a life of service. We kneel during prayers to show that we recognise God's sovereignty. And we may raise our hands during worship to show our openness to the Holy Spirit.

Yet when it comes to sermons, we revert to the purely verbal. Even if preachers simply copy three or four main headings onto overhead projector acetates and reveal them in turn, we remember them better. It's not just the fault of preachers that we forget sermons – at work we may take notes during seminars, but for some reason most of us choose not to make notes during Christian teaching. Some of your preachers may be excellent orators, but their messages may be even more effective with the addition of visual elements.

So why not encourage your preachers to make use of PowerPoint technology to reveal headings for different sections of the sermon, as well as suitable images? What about using drama to help illustrate particular points? Why not use visual aids to help the congregation understand the metaphor the preacher is making – why should it be just children who are helped in this way? If someone in your congregation has a testimony that neatly illustrates your point, why not ask them to give it as a living example of the abstract point you are trying to make?

How to do it:

1. Organise a get-together of your preaching team. Talk about the methods you use to communicate in sermons. Think about some oratorical skills such as the use of metaphor, stories and different headings. Could you learn from each other?

2. Now think of some of the visual stimuli you could use. What about visual aids, drama, PowerPoint presentations and testimonies?

3. Experiment with the use of these methods over several weeks. Collect feedback from the congregation. Did these methods help or hinder their understanding? Did they feel patronised or more engaged?

4. If necessary, your preachers may need further training in this area. If they take their teaching role seriously, they should have no problem accepting such help. Are there public speaking courses at your local college? Does your denomination run such courses? Are there resources you can buy that will help?

Further resources:

For more information on training for preachers in an audio-visual age, contact the College of Preachers, an ecumenical organisation devoted to improving sermons, on www.collegeofpreachers.org.uk; for information on drama resources, see: www.ridinglights.org or www.topcattheatre.com

52. Foster a word-of-mouth reputation for laying on 'special event' services.

Imagine members of your congregation are at work on a Monday morning. The inevitable question: 'Did you have a good weekend?' prompts them to tell incredulous work colleagues that their church replaced their normal Sunday service with worship in the local pub or park, a family pantomime or a meal for the local homeless community. It helps to subvert their expectations of what 'church' is actually like and helps to foster a reputation for your church as a place where anything could happen! The next time something like that happens, they might be persuaded to come along.

Of course, it wouldn't be right to replace your normal services with special events every week. But increasingly the model of 'Sunday worship' is becoming more fluid. The abandonment of Sunday as a day of rest has been well documented, and churches have often responded by organising midweek services. Business people may prefer to attend a short service in a city centre church during their lunch hour, and parents may prefer to bring their children to an after-school club that concludes with a short time of worship. So why not be more flexible on Sundays too?

It's good to provide 'seeker-friendly' events every so often that help to explain the gospel without necessarily expecting non-churchgoers to join in hymns and prayers expressing sentiments they don't believe in. So a morning service just before Christmas could be replaced with a family play based on the Nativity explaining why Jesus was born. An evening service could involve showing a current film with a relevant theme and discussing it afterwards. And something that helps to meet the needs of a particular group of people – a meal for the homeless or a seminar on parenting – might be something that non-regulars would feel more comfortable attending. It also shows how seriously you take the needs of your local community.

How to do it:

1. Consider your current diary of church services, and also your priorities in terms of mission and communication. What kind of groups are you trying to reach at present? Are the services you currently have planned likely to appeal to such groups?
2. Think about the possibility of replacing one service every couple of months with some kind of special event designed to appeal to families, young professionals, those on the fringe of church life or whoever you are looking to reach.
3. Experiment with different methods. Just because one method has worked well doesn't mean you need to do the same thing each time.
4. Encourage your congregation members to chat with their friends about what your church does. Create invitations and ask members of your congregation to give them away.

Weekly Leaflets

53. Revamp your weekly leaflet, using more graphics, bigger headings and more colour.

Many churches have a weekly leaflet or a single A4 sheet of information that they give to those who come to their services. Typically, this might give some information about that day's services and include details of forthcoming events or notices for congregation members. One of the biggest complaints churches have is that 'people don't read the leaflet'. The suggestion is that the information is clearly available, if only people would absorb it. Of course, part of the problem is that if churches use *only* their weekly leaflet to circulate important information, it's easy to overlook. The best way to ensure people know about such things is to use a *variety* of methods, one of which might be your weekly leaflet.

But it's true that some people only glance at their leaflet and hand it back at the end of the service, rather than taking it home and referring to it. One way to help people to absorb its contents more easily is to make it look livelier. Another is to make it easier to find your way around. If your church produces just one A4 sheet folded in half to make four A5-sized pages, you may wonder why people need such help. But items on a weekly leaflet are sometimes arranged so haphazardly that it's not easy to find things out quickly.

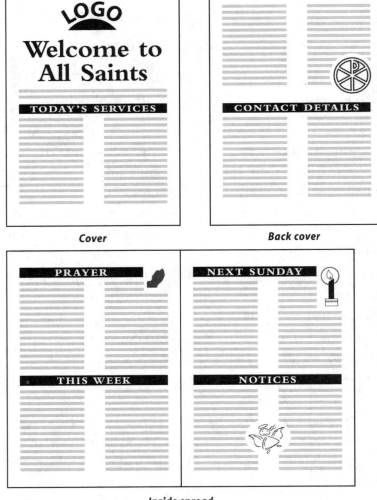

Cover   Back cover

Inside spread

How to do it:

1. Revamp the layout of your weekly leaflet, using proper or larger headings. Collect details about this week's services, including hymns, Bible readings, special liturgy, arrangements for Sunday school and so on, under the heading 'Today's Services'. Create a section on the week's activities titled 'This Week', and others entitled 'Forthcoming Events', 'Prayer Requests' and 'Contacts'. Make those headings as large as you can, as they function like headlines in a newspaper.

2. Avoid the temptation to use every single typeface in the computer. Use one font for the main text and another for headings. And don't try to squeeze as much text as possible on the page. If the information looks cramped and the font size has been reduced, it won't be easy to read.

3. Use graphics and symbols: a Bible reading might be denoted by an image of a Bible, prayer pointers by a pair of praying hands and so on. Clip-art can be used for this. Do include your church's logo too.

4. Place each section in a consistent order each week, so people know where to find what they want.

5. Provide a space for congregation members to make notes on the sermon, or print three or four of the main sermon headings and let people fill in the rest. If they have gone to the trouble of writing something down, they are less likely to leave the leaflet in church.

6. Experiment with ways of producing your leaflet that look more aesthetically pleasing, perhaps with the use of colour occasionally, and test the response.

7. Combine important notices on the weekly leaflets with other methods – verbal notices, posters and items in the church newsletter – rather than relying on this one method.

54. Send your weekly leaflet regularly to the local media.

If yours is the kind of church where there's often lots going on, you might simply not have the time to compose a press release each time something happens. One way to make sure that the local media keep abreast of activities in your church is to send them your parish magazine or church newsletter.

But sometimes things are organised too quickly to pre-view them in advance in a monthly or quarterly newsletter. It may be that the only way to let your congregation know quickly about them is to put the details in your weekly leaflet. Sending your weekly leaflets to the local media means they might also be able to respond, by phoning for more information. And something that might look relatively inconsequential to you might actually produce an interesting news story for the local media.

How to do it:

1. Send your weekly leaflet regularly to local newspapers and radio stations. If you can, send it to them as soon as it has been produced (perhaps on a Thursday or Friday), rather than waiting until after the relevant Sunday.

2. If you get some kind of response from reporters or if items appear in the newspaper or on the radio station as a result, keep on doing it. If not, re-assess whether it is worthwhile after a certain time.

Leaflets/Posters

55. Produce well-designed posters with attention-grabbing images, fewer words and more colour.

Weeks before the circus comes to your town, posters will appear on street corners, in shops and in parks advertising the fact. They are colourful and lively, showing images of clowns, acrobats or circus animals. You can't fail to notice them, and the anticipation of the circus's arrival is tangible. Now compare them with the posters that churches often use to publicise church events. Typically they will be smaller, photocopied in black and white, and contain all text and no images at all. You might find a few inside the church, and possibly one on the external noticeboard, but that might be it. Small wonder that few non-regulars realise something is happening.

In a consumer society full of well-designed logos, catchy slogans and expertly photographed images, our church's posters start off at a disadvantage. But we can help ourselves in a number of ways.

(i) Print posters professionally, and make them large.

If you can afford to print posters professionally, then do so. You are more likely to be able to use photographs, colours and eye-catching fonts. If you can only afford to print one set of posters professionally a year, then decide what your top priority is that year and print them for that event or activity. Colour posters catch the eye better, but you can also produce good results in one colour. And the bigger the posters are, the better.

(ii) Use an eye-catching image.

You'll need to find an image that conveys something of what your event involves. If you're holding a family fun day, use a photo of a happy child; if it's a Christmas carol service, use a photo of a chorister singing by candlelight; and if it's a well-known speaker, find a photo of him or her. Ideally, it should be a photo of a person or people, not a landscape, an abstract image, a line drawing or a photo of your church building. We all respond much better to images of people, which is why commercial firms use them. So use the expertise and market research of others to guide your thinking.

(iii) Cut down on text.

The fewer words you have, the bigger they can be, and the easier they will be to read. It also means that you can make the image as large as possible. Ideally, you should use the image to cover the entire poster and add the text over the top.

If you are also producing leaflets about the same event, it's helpful for the design of posters and leaflets to be the same (i.e. use the same image, the same typeface, similar text and so on). That helps people to connect the leaflet that may come through their letterbox with the poster they have seen elsewhere.

Finding good places to put posters involves a lot of hard work. If you have produced them professionally, you will have paid for several hundred copies to make it worthwhile. Give several to each of your congregation members to put in their front windows, workplaces, schools, cars and so on. Then recruit a team that can take the posters around your community.

How to do it:

1. Consult with your communications team as to which events are your priorities. Decide to get posters for those events professionally printed.
2. Find an image that effectively sums up the event. It should be a photo of a person or people, perhaps from a previous event of a similar nature. It needn't necessarily have been taken at your church.
3. Take the image and the text you would like to a professional printer. Design the poster alongside the printer. If you can afford it, ask for it to be printed in colour. If you can, print the text on top of the image, and print both as large as possible. Remember to use your church's logo. See www.getyourchurchnoticed.com.
4. If you are also printing leaflets, give both posters and leaflets a consistent design.
5. Distribute the posters as widely as possible, using congregation members' own homes. You may need to discover which of your congregation members live on main roads and which on cul-de-sacs. Use your larger posters in places where they are more likely to be seen.
6. Recruit a team to take posters to places such as retailers, community centres, libraries, GPs' surgeries, local authority offices and tourist information centres. They will need to ask permission from the relevant people in each place, but make sure they are armed with drawing pins, Blu-Tack and Sellotape to hang up their posters. Ask them to make a note of which locations gave permission for posters to be hung up.

56. Create professionally produced A3-sized posters to publicise events on church noticeboards.

In the section on external noticeboards, we saw how important it is to keep changing displays regularly to grab the attention of passers-by. So when you produce posters, make sure they are large enough to display in the glass-fronted section of your main external noticeboard. If you've printed hundreds of A4 posters, you may also need to get some A3-sized ones done so the details can be seen by drivers and passers-by. That should also give you a stock of larger posters for other prominent places in your community.

If you can only afford to get A4 posters printed, one option is to fill the glass-fronted section of your external noticeboard with four identical A4 posters all pinned up together. Passers-by won't be able to read them so easily, but at least the importance of that single event is emphasised.

How to do it:

1. If the posters that you are producing are not A3-sized already, try to have some A3 posters printed as well for your external noticeboard.
2. The other option is to fill your external noticeboard with four (or more) A4 posters.
3. Keep changing those posters regularly, as the events you are publicising happen. This could be another role for your poster co-ordinator.

57. Produce leaflets publicising your church's forthcoming events or activities.

Leaflets and posters have different functions. Leaflets are designed to be taken away by individuals, and may contain more detailed information than a poster ever could. They can be thought of as complementary: someone glances at a poster and realises something is happening; then they see a leaflet publicising the same event or activity and take one away. That's why it's important for both posters and leaflets to have a consistent design.

If your communications team has decided on its priorities and you are professionally printing posters for one or more of your most important events, it makes sense to produce leaflets at the same time. They can be A5-sized leaflets, with a scaled-down version of the poster on one side, and more detailed information overleaf. Or they can be A4-sized leaflets, folded twice to make a bookmark-sized leaflet. Such leaflets should be produced in plenty of time before the event.

The thinking behind the design of posters also applies to leaflets. Just because you have more space to include detailed information doesn't mean you should try to fit in as much text as possible. Use a mixture of images and text. Use colours and headings. And do remember the importance of 'white space' – leaving enough space between different blocks of text so people can read them more easily.

When publicising special events, churches have a habit of leaving leaflets at the back of church and hoping congregation members will pick them up. In today's fast-moving society, we often don't respond to things unless they are literally pushed in our faces. If your event is a top priority and you want people to know about it, make sure every member of your congregation has the information at their fingertips. That might mean handing out leaflets to every person as they enter or leave church. It might even mean giving out handfuls of leaflets to each person for them to distribute to family, friends and in their streets. It should also involve you leaving piles of leaflets in places such as community centres, libraries, council offices and GPs' surgeries.

Churches may be quite good at recognising the need for leaflets publicising events. But often the publicity for specific activities within the church (youth group, mothers and toddlers group etc.) is left to the group concerned. Your communications team may want to think about this: if your priority during the next few months is outreach to families, it's important to make sure family activities are publicised, using leaflets without accompanying posters. Make sure they include photos of the activity in action. These leaflets can be given out by individual members of the group concerned to friends or left in a suitable place – information about parents' groups can be given to schools to display, for instance.

If you can't afford to have leaflets printed professionally very often, you can buy packs of generic Christmas or Easter leaflets (and accompanying posters) from organisations such as CPO (Christian Publishing and Outreach). They include spaces so you can photocopy details of your church's services onto the back or inside of what are usually well-produced leaflets.

How to do it:

1. Check your church's priorities with your communications team. Are any special events planned for which posters will be produced? Decide whether you can also produce leaflets professionally.
2. Try to make sure leaflets are designed in a similar way to your posters, using the same images, typefaces and so on.
3. In designing leaflets, remember the importance of colour, headings, white space and the minimum of text.
4. Hand out leaflets to each member of your congregation, ask them to distribute them, and leave piles of leaflets in public places.
5. Consider whether you need to publicise activities in the same way.

Further resources:

For more information about posters and leaflets produced by Christian Publishing and Outreach, see: www.cpo-online.org.uk

58. Create specifically youth-friendly flyers for youth events.

If you regularly go to nightclubs, you'll soon become familiar with the 'club flyer' style of design, publicising their special events. It's quite hard to describe – they are often printed on A6-sized cards that are colourful, with an abstract design. The fonts used are often unusual, with exclusively lower case lettering and deliberate misspellings common. This style clearly marks out such flyers from other kinds of publicity. (See www.getyourchurchnoticed.com)

If you want to put on some kind of youth event, or if you want to advertise your youth group, the normal style of leaflet outlined above may elicit little interest among youngsters. A sense of style and design is perhaps more important among teenagers than the rest of the population. If your youth group say they 'wouldn't be caught dead' with your church's leaflets, it's probably the design that's at fault. But if you can replicate the style of club flyers, you might actually get teenagers interested.

It's probably a good idea to involve your church's youngsters in helping to design such publicity. They'll have a much better idea about what styles are in and out. They'll also be more inclined to dish out leaflets they've helped to design than ones you've designed for them. If anything, the importance of getting a professional to finish the design and print these flyers is even greater. Anything that looks as though it was churned off on the church photocopier won't be taken seriously.

How to do it:

1. Collect examples of club flyers. Ask your youth group to show you examples, or collect some from local nightclubs.
2. Ask for the help of your youth group in creating publicity for youth events, services or activities.
3. Ask a professional to take those ideas and create a design. Bring the design back to your youth group before

going ahead and printing it. Try to print the design on
A6-sized cards to replicate club flyers.

4. Give out handfuls of these cards to your church youngsters so they can invite their friends.

5. Depending on the type of event, such cards can be given
   out at secondary schools, in town centres, or even outside nightclubs themselves.

59. Create a 'term card' showing the themes and styles of church services and activities for the next few months.

If yours is the kind of church where there's lots going on,
it's easy for congregation members to miss things. Your

efforts to publicise the larger, high profile events such as the children's holiday club or Alpha course may pay dividends. But it's the slightly lower profile events that people might miss a reference to.

Yet the church leadership is likely to have some idea of what's happening when. There should be a definitive church diary somewhere. Why not share the details of what's happening when with the rest of the congregation? A monthly diary might be printed anyway in the parish magazine or church newsletter. If so, perhaps what's needed is something that details what's happening on Sundays and other significant occasions for the next three to six months. This is especially valuable if the styles of worship you use each Sunday don't follow a set pattern each month.

This is called a 'term card' simply because churches in university towns and cities often produce such a card detailing events during the next academic term. Churchgoers are often busy people, with the normal round of holidays, weekends away and work commitments on top of church meetings. Anything that might help them to plan in advance is valuable. They may even choose not to go away one weekend because a particular sermon series is so riveting!

Typically, a term card might include details of the style of services (Communion, family service, Iona service, healing service etc.) each Sunday, who is preaching and on what subject, and other significant social, spiritual or evangelistic midweek events. It's fine to produce such a card on a church photocopier. How often you produce a card depends on how far your church's leadership plans in advance, but your church may be following a certain theme for several

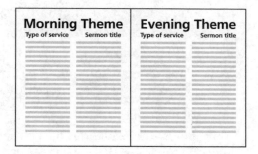

months, and you may want to produce a card detailing the entire series of services.

There is a danger that people can develop a 'consumer' mentality – coming to the styles of service they like and avoiding the ones they don't. They may even be fussy about which preachers they like. But they may do this whether you have a term card or not, and simply make those decisions on a week-to-week basis. Hopefully the act of making more information available will ensure that churchgoers don't miss events, and it will help them know when would be most appropriate to invite friends. The cards can, of course, also be distributed to non-regulars.

How to do it:

1. Your church leadership will probably plan Sunday services well in advance. Discover how this process happens and how often your church could produce a term card.
2. Collate details of Sunday services and other important events happening within that 'term'.
3. Produce a term card, typically with details of what's

happening at each Sunday morning and evening service. Print it on the church photocopier. Include your church's logo and contact details.

4. Give copies out to members of your congregation at a couple of Sunday services. Have copies available at the back of church.

5. Put copies into welcome packs that are going to be distributed around your neighbourhood (see Ideas 39–42). If you can distribute term cards by themselves at libraries, community centres and other public places, do so.

6. If you notice that people are actively avoiding certain styles of worship or certain preachers, it may be a good time to review that worship style or the gifts of that preacher! If you are confident that that style of service or that preacher should continue, you might want to review the idea of term cards.

Parish Magazine

60. Ask your congregation to subsidise your church publication as a form of outreach.

If you knew a way of communicating to individuals across the country, combining a consistent, nationwide set of underlying principles with a unique focus on people's immediate communities, then marketing companies might beg to know your secret. But that's exactly what we have in the Church – a national template for belief that is localised in individual communities. Our church publications can reflect the coherence of those beliefs with a focus on issues, events and activities in the immediate locality.

Not every worshipping community has its own magazine or newsletter. If not, it might be time to consider launching one. Churches that do have their own publication usually underestimate its potential. Perhaps it is only distributed to those who already go to church and a few others with previous links. Perhaps it only includes articles that appeal to those with an attachment to the faith. Perhaps the fact that it is photocopied makes it look dull and amateur compared to secular, colour glossy magazines. These are just some of the reasons that churchgoers and non-churchgoers don't read church magazines avidly.

The sad thing is that something that could be such a powerful tool for outreach can be seen, at its worst, as a burden on those who put it together, and, even at its best, as a harmless publication that's largely irrelevant to the local community. That can be because little thought has gone into its purpose. It's simply produced because it always has been. But embracing its potential as a valuable tool for outreach could involve revamping it beyond recognition.

In some churches, it's assumed that the magazine will make money – through advertising and subscriptions. If money is tight, fundraising can become its raison d'être. Time and energy spent on securing adverts from local firms can mean less time and energy is spent on the content. Congregation members may subscribe to it out of habit or duty, rather than because they are attracted by its content. So it's no surprise that they sometimes don't read it properly.

If you want to make your magazine an effective communication tool, it's important that you tackle its purpose and its finances first. If you want to get your church publication noticed within your local community, your congregation needs to understand that its primary aim should be outreach. It should be freed from any restrictions imposed on it by having to make money. In fact, if a publication is genuinely understood as a powerful mission tool, it might be more appropriate to subsidise it – devoting some of the church's outreach budget towards improving it without expecting any return at all.

For one thing, if you are trying to reach people in the wider community – perhaps by putting information through people's letterboxes – it's difficult to charge them for it. After all, it's the church that wants them to have this information. Why would they pay for it if they haven't chosen to receive it? And it would seem churlish to charge the 'regular' readership for it if you are giving it away free to others.

Of course, the idea that a magazine might be a method of outreach may also be a new one. The purpose of any publication you already have might be simply to 'keep church members informed' or something similar. But when a congregation aims the content of its magazine at the non-churchgoer, with an attractive design and wide distribution, it often becomes a must-read for church members too. Part of this may be simply that greater thought has gone into the way in which information is communicated – in-jokes are banned, church jargon is explained and it's assumed that people don't know the background to issues. Part of it may also be a better use of photos, better design, and more closely edited articles.

How to do it:

1. Talk to the people who edit your current publication. What do they see as its purpose? And how is it financed?
2. If their vision is along the lines of 'informing church-goers about church activities', ask both them and your church's leadership team whether they would like to expand the vision.
3. If your magazine is financed by advertising and is expected to make a profit, talk to your editors and your church's leadership about how this affects the prospects of it being used as a mission tool.

4. Decide how you would like to go forward. Would you like to expand its readership? Revamp its design? Use it to help reach non-churchgoers in the community? Use more or better photos? Switch to an improved printing process? The chances are that it will have to be subsidised rather than contributing to your church's finances.

5. Consider the content of your publication. If you are aiming it specifically at non-churchgoers, what elements of your current magazine would you need to jettison, and what new features or news items should you include? (See Ideas 61–66.)

6. Consider the production process. If your church subsidises the publication, would it be possible to print it professionally rather than photocopy it? (See Idea 67.)

7. It is possible, in the long-term, for a successful church publication to make money, either through adverts or subscriptions. But the key is to make it successful (i.e. widely read!) *first*. Then, once it has become a must-read in your locality, firms will want to advertise their products in it and readers may be persuaded to start paying a modest cover price.

61. Re-launch your parish magazine as a community newsletter and invite non-churchgoers to write for it.

Another common misconception is that a church publication should be a 'magazine' – a monthly collection of articles written by church members about their experiences, their faith or a particular issue. What often happens is that an editor struggles to find people within the congregation with the confidence to write about weighty matters, and the magazine becomes a collection of articles about people's trips abroad, favourite recipes, recollections of bygone days or reflections on recent church events. That's not to say there isn't a place for some of those things in a church publication. But it's easy to see why someone who isn't part of that worshipping community wouldn't be interested in recipes or reflections from someone they've never met. Sometimes any remaining spaces are filled with 'fillers' from a national church news service. There's nothing wrong with having a national perspective, but such items do run counter to the unique selling point of your church's publication – its localness.

Perhaps it would be better to use a different word to describe your church's publication. 'Newsletter' is a better word because it suggests something short, snappy and full of what is about to happen. It's no coincidence that national and local media are obsessed with what will happen next, rather than what has just happened. It's because they know that that is what we're interested in. 'News' is, by definition, what's new, and what's next. Unfortunately, our church magazines are often too busy reflecting on something that may have happened months ago by the time the magazine comes out.

If we genuinely want to revamp our church publications so they are more widely read, let's think of them as newsletters that tell readers information they wouldn't otherwise know. So May's edition should be full of the exciting things that will happen in and around your church in May and June. This information might be 'hot off the press' simply because the organisers have only just agreed what will happen in time for your deadline. This helps to make your publication essential reading for both church-goers and non-churchgoers.

The other way of expanding your readership and emphasising the localness of your publication is to combine church and community news in one newsletter. This serves a number of purposes. First, it actually offers a service to your local community if it doesn't have its own publication already. Offering a way of disseminating information is a way of putting your church at the heart of the community it serves. Secondly, it encourages greater interest in your publication, as the various community groups and individuals featured will want to read it. Thirdly, it offers the chance for those producing the magazine to develop relationships with the organisers of secular activities in your community. Those links may be useful when it comes to working in partnership with secular organisations on community issues.

Some church newsletters have done this and eventually evolved into full-blown secular publications run by the community that may or may not include church news. Obviously this isn't your aim. But it's interesting how quickly successful publications can be 'taken over' by the community in this way – and how a change of editor can suddenly jeopardise a church's chances of getting its own news printed. If necessary, you may have to write some kind of 'constitution' or founding principles that make clear that this is a church publication within which church news should always have a place.

How to do it:

1. Discuss whether you need to turn your 'magazine' into a 'newsletter' to emphasise a change of ethos from reflecting on past events to previewing forthcoming events.

2. If you want to re-launch your publication as a newsletter, that may involve a change of layout or format. Church magazines are often in A5 format, with similar covers each month. A newsletter is most commonly in an A4 format, with a 'masthead' or title at the top of page one, with the rest of the page devoted to the most important news story of the month.

3. Choose a month when lots of news is likely to be happening for your launch edition.

4. Ensure your editor liaises closely with your church's leadership, so that he or she knows about things that are planned as far in advance as possible. Encourage your editor to think in terms of telling people things they won't already know.

5. Start to make links with community leaders, those who run voluntary groups, councillors, MPs and other local organisations. Tell them that you are happy to include their news within your publication, as space allows and as appropriate. Once you start to publish their information, they will be encouraged to send more.

6. Expand your distribution network to cover the organisations whose news you are printing. So you may be able to send copies to parents via your local school, place copies in your local library or GPs' surgery or give them away at your community centre's open day.

7. If necessary, make sure there is some kind of 'constitution' to fall back on to make sure your publication
doesn't evolve into an exclusively secular newsletter.

62. Create a single ecumenical publication.

If you are expanding your publication to include news from
local community organisations, you will probably also
approach churches of other denominations and make the
same offer to them. If they don't produce a publication
themselves, they may be grateful. But if every church
already produces something, don't despair – this could create a good opportunity to work together.

We have already explored how church unity can be
emphasised by working together under a common identity
or logo (Idea 8). The magazine or newsletter is a good, practical way of putting this into action. If your local population
sees churches of all denominations working together on a
single, ecumenical publication, it's a powerful symbol of
unity. It emphasises that different denominations are all
part of the same team rather than competing with each other.

The other advantage is that the churches involved can
pool their resources. Rather than six different churches
with six different editors and publications, there would just
be one. The six editors could become an effective editorial
team, hopefully with complementary skills, rather than
working individually. And the resultant publication could
use the budget of all six previous publications put together.
There would also be advantages in terms of distribution
within the community, which could be shared. And the
content of the publication itself would help Baptists to

know what was happening at the local Methodist church, and so on.

Of course, different churches have different emphases. But if the aim for all the churches involved was one of outreach, the editorial team should be able to agree that anything that seemed too 'churchy' or too denominational should be excluded.

How to do it:

1. Investigate what your neighbouring churches do in terms of newsletters or publications. If no other churches publish anything to the wider community, invite them to contribute to your newsletter.

2. If other churches do already publish something, ask other church leaders if they would be open to sharing resources and creating a joint publication.

3. Encourage your editor to work alongside editors from other denominations, perhaps on some kind of editorial team. Invite them to produce some guidelines for deciding what kind of content to include in any joint publication. Ideally, it would be good to mix up all the church news throughout the publication, rather than having separate pages for separate churches. This helps to emphasise your unity.

4. Look at how to pool the financial resources that you have to achieve economies of scale. Perhaps, by working together, you can finally afford a professional printer. And perhaps, because you will be producing more copies of the newsletter, it will actually be more cost-effective to get it done professionally.

5. Investigate how to pool your distribution network to avoid duplication. Different churches might offer to distribute to those streets, community centres, schools and libraries nearest to them.

63. Encourage your editor to edit.

It might seem an odd trait to encourage in a Christian, but editors of church newsletters or magazines often need to develop a more ruthless streak. Many editors of church publications don't really operate as 'editors' at all, but as 'collators'. They collect articles from contributors and insert the text into pages without editing it at all. That can be because they know the writers and don't want to risk offending them by altering or rejecting their text. Or perhaps the editor doesn't feel confident of improving it by re-writing it.

This is understandable, of course, in a small worshipping community. The problem with this approach is that you're entirely dependent on what you're given. The 2,000-word feature about someone's visit to Jerusalem ends up across pages 1–4, starting with superfluous details about how comfy the plane seats were, what the in-flight meal was and so on. Yet the Alpha supper, which is specifically designed for non-churchgoers, only gets a brief mention on the second-last page. If the editor thought about his readership, he might realise that the latter should be given a higher priority. The way to make sure this priority is reflected in the publication is by imaginative editing.

Editors edit on behalf of their readers, *not* on behalf of those who contribute articles. They do this in a number of ways:

(i) They **reject some contributions** as unsuitable. Not every article submitted will be appropriate for your publication, especially if it is a newsletter with a specifically evangelistic focus. That thrilling short story, evocative poem or reflection on a spiritual theme might be perfect for some other publication, but not yours. It obviously helps if the editor has a clear idea what he or she wants to achieve in the publication, as that makes it easier to justify decisions.

(ii) A good editor will **commission some stories** or be proactive in researching and writing them. If the communications team has decided there will be a focus on ministry to the bereaved, the editor shouldn't wait until someone else thinks about writing a piece on it. He or she should approach those involved in that work and either ask them to write a piece themselves or talk to them about the work and write it for them. Or perhaps your editor could recruit a 'reporter' whose job it is to do the research and writing while the editor concentrates on the editing and design work.

(iii) Editors help **make a story easier to understand**, which can involve rewriting whole pieces, or at least changing the way they start. Those who aren't used to writing often do so chronologically. A story about a trip abroad will typically begin: 'It was a lovely, sunny morning as we set off at 7.30am to go to Heathrow. . . .' By the time the reader has worked their way through details of the actual journey, their eyes have glazed over.

A good editor will alter the start to tell the reader why they should be interested in reading what follows, ideally by both emphasising the local links and signalling what the rest of the article is about (for instance: 'Lucy Jones normally teaches 11-year-olds at Anytown Secondary School, but for a week she took part in a unique project to teach Israeli and Palestinian children side by side. . .').

If the editor continues to rewrite the story by expanding on the details of the most important aspects of the story, they may end up rewriting the whole thing. They may also have discarded parts of the original that were superfluous. Undoubtedly it will be a better story for having been through this process.

They can also remove church jargon or complicated references, or explain something where the writer has assumed knowledge that the reader won't have. It helps if the editor also has an idea of the tastes of those living near your church – are they more likely to be *Sun* readers or *Daily Telegraph* readers? That means the style of the article can be tailored to fit your local readership.

(iv) The **tone of stories** is also important. If you decide to focus on the parent-and-toddler group, the editor could visit the group, talk to those who currently attend and write an article describing the atmosphere and activities, including quotes from parents whose children enjoy it. That approach is likely to result in a friendly, informative story. If the editor asks the leaders of the group to write something themselves, it's more likely to be about the organisation and structure of the group than the atmosphere generated, because that's their focus as leaders. And, because of their natural humility, the leaders are less likely to say how good the group is. A good editor will be able to rewrite contributions so they fit in with the friendly, conversational tone of the rest of the newsletter.

(v) A good editor also has an idea about the **positioning of stories**. Most people know the front page is the place where newspapers put their top story. Yet many magazine editors persist in putting the vicar's letter there, whether or not he or she has anything interesting to say. Fewer people will realise that pages 3, 5 and 7, the centre pages and the back page are also important. Choose carefully which stories go where, as the reader will subconsciously understand that the stories on these pages are the most important for your church to communicate.

(vi) And the **length of stories** is key. If your church leadership or communications team has decided that this year's focus should be on young people, or if you have an important, once-a-year evangelistic opportunity coming up, surely that should be the longest piece in the newsletter? That might involve pruning some other stories radically – and it could involve asking for more information about your top priority.

Don't worry about the idea of pruning stories drastically. Professional journalists deliberately write their stories with the most important information first, so the final few paragraphs can be removed without losing anything too important. If your editor has done their job properly in the rewriting process described above, they should also be able to shorten stories considerably.

Some editors may feel uncomfortable doing this, because they don't want to offend those who write articles. But most contributors make no claim to having writing skills and actually welcome such editing. And if the editing process is made clear beforehand, few people are likely to be offended.

How to do it:

1. Encourage your editor to read national and local newspapers with an analytical eye. How do they phrase things, especially at the start of stories, to encourage the reader to continue to read that story? Encourage them to think about how they could reword some of the contributions they have received for the church publication in the same way.

2. Send your editor on a training course, such as those run nationally by the denominations in the UK.

3. Encourage your editor to be ruthless. And make sure the rest of your congregation are aware of the policy on contributions so they won't be offended if theirs is rewritten or rejected.

4. If your editor finds problems with this approach, make your minister the final arbiter in any major decision about whether an article appears or how it might be rewritten. That gives added weight to the decision. Once the editor gets the hang of how such decisions should be taken, he or she may feel more confident about making them.

5. Survey your congregation to see if they have noticed an improvement in the publication. If they have, it will give added justification for this approach.

Further resources:

Training courses in magazine editing are arranged jointly by the main UK church denominations. See: www. commstraining.org.uk for details. Your local diocese or district may also offer similar training.

64. Include stories of faith from your congregation in your publication.

Think about the way you read newspapers and magazines. Do you start at page 1 and read every word until you get to the end? Or do you flick through pages, waiting for your eye to alight on a story or a photo about someone you have heard of? What about the way a TV news programme or documentary examines a health story? Usually, they would focus on a particular patient (e.g. 'Every fortnight Norman Smith comes into hospital for chemotherapy. This new drug means he won't need to.').

Most people are interested in stories about other people. We tend to access stories about abstract things by focusing on one person affected by it. At a national level, this can mean a focus on an issue by referring to a celebrity or soap character who has just experienced a messy divorce, sudden bereavement or the birth of a baby with learning disabilities.

Now think about how we communicate abstract issues such as faith in our publications. Too often, we plunge straight into spiritual issues without thinking about applying them to real life. The chances are that Christians and non-Christians alike will be able to think more clearly about answered prayer, faith in the workplace or Christian healing if they are given concrete examples. Telling stories of how faith affects normal people's lives is an incredibly powerful way to get your point across – partly because telling a story isn't 'preaching' at people. If your newsletter is aimed at non-churchgoers, this may be virtually the only way to talk about spiritual issues.

There is another reason for this. Think about how a local newspaper packs the names and photos of as many people as it can into its pages. That's because they hope everyone who is featured will buy copies. Your church's newsletter is even more local than such a newspaper. So if you feature someone from your congregation, then their family, friends, neighbours and work colleagues may also want to read about their experiences. If others come across a story about someone they recognise, they'll keep reading. Do make sure you include a photo, as they may recognise the face rather than the name.

How to do it:

1. Some Christians are more comfortable talking about their faith than others. Partly this is to do with what kind of church they go to – some encourage people to tell their testimonies regularly, others prefer faith to be a more private matter. Your church leadership might need to emphasise the value of sharing with others about how God has worked in our lives.

2. Suggest to your editor that this could be a regular, prominent feature in your publication. It might be something that your editor delegates to a reporter who will interview someone different for each edition.

3. Find someone in your congregation who is happy to talk about their faith. It needn't be some miraculous healing or 50 years of missionary service. It could simply be the story about how they first started coming to church, or how a simple prayer was answered, or how their faith affects their work.

4. Ask the person if they would like to be interviewed. Your editor or reporter should chat to them, write an article based on the interview and – ideally – show it to the subject of the interview before it appears.

5. Your editor should ensure there is a photo of the person being interviewed.

6. Once such a feature has appeared once, and people know what is involved, it should be easier to recruit others to take part.

7. If appropriate, you could also use such stories of faith on your website.

65. Recruit someone to take good-quality photographs.

Examine virtually any secular magazine or newspaper, and you'll find that it's full of photographs. On the 'beauty' pages of a women's magazine, you'll see photos of the cosmetic products being used. On a newspaper's sports pages, there will be photos of the footballer referred to – even if you are well aware of what he looks like. It's what helps to draw us in to reading a particular story, as well as breaking up slabs of unattractive grey text.

Now look at your church publication. Are there similar photos to catch the eye? Or would the casual browser flick through your magazine from start to finish without seeing any images to draw them into the text? The adage about a picture being worth a thousand words is true – even if your publication is full of interesting stories about people's faith or church and community activities, it will be the photos that persuade browsers to read them.

These days, digital photography and desk-top publishing packages mean it is incredibly easy to take photos, transfer them from your camera to your computer screen, and design them into a page. Yet, incredibly, some editors working with sophisticated desk-top publishing software use no photos at all. Some use line drawings, especially if the magazine is photocopied and they feel that photos simply wouldn't be copied adequately. Any images are obviously better than none, but so few other institutions use such line drawings that they can make your church seem incredibly dated.

How to do it:

1. Most congregations include at least one person with a good-quality digital or SLR (single-lens reflex) camera. Try to recruit them to take photos for your publication.
2. If no one is available, perhaps your church could buy a decent digital camera for your editor to use. It might only cost a couple of hundred pounds, but could transform your publication.
3. You might have to consider changing your production process at the same time as including photos in your publication. Perhaps it's time for your editor to switch to a better desk-top publishing package, or for you to

abandon the church photocopier and try using a professional printer (see Idea 67).

4. Some editors with limited circulations use colour photos on certain pages of an otherwise photocopied publication, simply by printing off each colour page individually on their computer's colour printer. These are then inserted into the rest of the publication before stapling. This is possible in the short-term, but it may prove to be expensive and time-consuming.

5. If decent photos have been taken, persuade your editor to use them as large as you can within the constraints of your publication.

6. In time, your editor will have a 'library' of photos of all sorts of church activities and of people within your congregation. Your editor should store the photos logically so that he or she can use the same photos to illustrate future stories.

Further resources:

Training courses in taking and using digital photos are arranged jointly by the main UK church denominations. See: www.commstraining.org.uk for details.

66. Revamp your design.

Professional graphic designers must be busier than ever these days. So much information – posters, leaflets, billboards, magazines and websites – is so well designed that we only notice it when we see something that isn't of such high quality. Subconsciously, we think the contents of that leaflet, poster or magazine will be less important, as less thought seems to have gone into it.

Design and layout of a newsletter or magazine is, of course, a specialist art, and there's no reason why your current editor should be an expert. Training and experience may be needed. But here are a few pointers.

(i) Think about the **size of your newsletter**. It is possible to create an immaculately designed magazine or newsletter in A5 or A3 formats, but an A4 format does give you the flexibility you need without the publication becoming too unwieldy.

(ii) Design usually takes place by **using columns**. There's a reason why newspapers and magazines organise their text into columns. The human eye can scan the width of a column at one go, so text organised in columns can easily be read by simply moving the eye downwards. Columns that are too wide can create problems – the reader may get to the end of a line stretching right across an A4 page and then, momentarily, be unable to find the start of the next line.

If you are using an A5 format, you can only really divide the page into two columns. With an A4 page, you can have three columns on each page. Photos can be spread over two or three columns and an article covering two columns can sit next to a single-column story. In a double-page centrespread you have six columns to play with.

(iii) You might want to think about the **style of font** you use for text. Some amateur editors seem to want to show off every single font in their computer. The result can look incredibly confusing. Different fonts have different characters – some look warm and friendly, others look either old-fashioned or avant garde. Find one, or possibly two, to use for your main text – Arial, Verdana, Trebuchet or Times New Roman is fine. Then find two or three different fonts to use for your head-lines – a bold or black font usually works best. Use those fonts consistently, and your publication will soon develop a 'house style'.

(iv) How the **text flows** is important. Look at any news-paper or magazine and you'll see the text running from left to right and from the top to the bottom of the page. If a story starts on column one halfway down the page and it runs into a second or third column, the text in those subsequent columns won't appear at the top of the page – it will be level with or below where the first column started. Again, this makes it easier to fol-low the story.

(v) **White space** is helpful too. One of the most common mistakes that editors make is trying to squeeze all the text into the space available. It often makes the page look too cluttered. Space around the text, between the text and the photo and between the text and headline can make the design look 'cleaner'.

(vi) Almost without exception, amateur editors use **head-lines** that are too small. They might be tucked away at the top of a page, perhaps only a couple of point sizes bigger than the text itself. The point of headlines is to draw the eye to the story, but it's difficult to do that if they are too small. There's nothing wrong with taking over a quarter or a third of the page with the headline for the story.

Headlines also have another function. The size of the headline (along with the length of the story) is an indication of its importance. If your design is sufficiently flexible to have several stories on each page, the longest, and hopefully most important, story should have the largest headline. The tiny filler at the bottom of the page will have the smallest. The front-page story should have the largest headline of all.

(vii) It's already been mentioned that **photos** should be used as large as possible. It's worth repeating here, partly because the best designers actually design their pages (and even edit their stories) around their photos, rather than trying to squeeze them in after placing the text on the page. Bear in mind that it will be the photo and headline that draw the reader into the text, so make sure your photos are as prominent as they can be.

Desk-top publishing software has helped to make design easier. It's possible to shuffle things around a page before settling on the favoured design. It's important to pay particular attention to the front page, as this is the chance to make a good first impression. Your editor should already be earmarking this page for the best story, with the biggest headline. Encourage them also to use their best photo here, which may or may not be linked to the best story.

How to do it:

1. If your editor is still using scissors, paper and glue to put together your church publication, it's unlikely to be

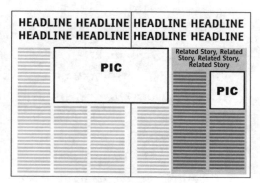

making much of an impact on the local community. Suggest that investing in some kind of desk-top publishing software will make an enormous difference.

2. Offer your editor some training in how to use their new or current software to its full potential. Local colleges may be able to offer suitable courses.

3. Ask your editor to come up with a few sample designs of page layout, including sample front pages, back pages and centrespreads, using different combinations of column width, headline size and style of font – perhaps even experimenting with different page sizes. Ask your communications team to examine these and choose what looks best. Encourage your editor to use the chosen design consistently throughout the publication.

4. Ask your communications team to periodically review the design of the publication.

Further resources:

Training courses in magazine design are arranged jointly by the main UK church denominations. See: www. commstraining.org.uk for details.

67. Improve the production of your publication.

Such is the quality of much of the literature that we see these days that the black and white, photocopied parish magazine can look incredibly dated. The content is almost irrelevant, as the look of the publication already communicates something loud and clear about your church.

Not every church will be able to afford to produce a professionally printed, colour, glossy publication each month. But maybe you could do so three or four times a year. Would it actually be a more effective use of your resources to publish a newsletter that looks more professional, but less frequently? Another option might be to cut down on the number of pages you produce, but to make sure that your slimmed-down newsletter is produced professionally. Cutting the number of pages you produce might actually help to force your editor to edit contributions anyway (see Idea 63). Either way, a better-looking magazine is more likely to be retained by churchgoers and non-churchgoers alike. If it's going to be read more closely than your existing one, this approach might pay dividends.

Another approach might be to work towards a better-looking publication, but in stages. If your existing magazine is duplicated, why not consider photocopying? If it's already photocopied, why not consider producing a colour front and back page? If you already do that, why not find out how much it would cost to get the inside pages professionally printed in black and white? This particular switch is something worth paying extra for because it can transform your photographs from looking like photocopied black splodges into recognisable images. These images are key, so it's worth getting them right. And if your publication is already printed professionally in black and white, why not find out how much some extra colour would cost?

How to do it:

1. Examine how your publication is produced at the moment. What are the advantages and disadvantages of doing it this way?

2. Research how much it might cost to improve its production quality. Could this cost be subsidised by your church?

3. If your church's resources are tight, would it be possible to produce a publication less frequently, or with fewer pages, to bring down the costs? Compare the advantages of a better-looking and more tightly edited publication with the disadvantages of less frequent communication or fewer pages to play with.

4. Examine the option of working with churches of other denominations to produce a joint publication that looks better than any of your individual efforts (see Idea 62).

68. Create a more effective distribution system to ensure your publication reaches as many people as possible.

Most church publications depend on voluntary help to a greater or lesser extent – editors in particular will give up a lot of their spare time. And most churches are reliant on a distribution system that involves congregation members taking piles of magazines to post through the letterboxes of readers who don't come to church.

If your church has tried to improve the content, design and production of your church publication, it makes sense to try and distribute it as far afield as possible. And if the purpose of the publication is specifically evangelistic, it makes no sense to restrict its circulation to church members. But churches often find it difficult to hurdle the problem of distribution, especially as it seems difficult enough to

persuade church members to distribute the existing magazine to the handful of housebound people or others who
retain links with the church.

First, if the congregation understands the purpose of a
newsletter to be outreach, and if the newsletter is of high
quality, there is likely to be greater enthusiasm for its distribution. If they are proud of its content and design, they are
more likely to volunteer to put it through the letterboxes of
their neighbours. Success breeds success, so if an event has
been publicised in this way, and draws a big crowd, church
members will be more eager to distribute details of the next
one. Secondly, as already mentioned, if you improve its
production, you may need to reduce its frequency. Fewer
editions means fewer distribution runs.

It's also possible to increase the circulation gradually, perhaps by focusing on specific types of reader. If your latest
edition features the local church school prominently, it's
probably worth asking the headteacher if the publication
can be distributed via the school to parents. If it features the
local football team, community organisation or scout group,
you can do the same thing. But don't do it as a one-off – ask
if you can continue to regularly distribute it this way. This
is obviously easier if you are regularly including news about
that organisation within your pages.

Or you could focus on a particular part of your locality.
What about a concerted attempt to reach young families
who live on a new estate, combined with a series of articles
about your family services or after-school club? Or a focus
on the streets nearest your church building if you are
emphasising in your newsletter that the church is open
24/7 for prayer? It may be a good aim to try eventually to

distribute it to every home in your neighbourhood, but you might have to work up gradually to doing this.

How to do it:

1. Ensure your congregation realises the importance of your publication in outreach to the local community. Encourage them to get involved in its distribution as a 'non-threatening' form of evangelism.
2. Consider the frequency of publication, perhaps in tandem with improvements to its production.
3. Think how you can link features within your publication with opportunities for wider distribution. Make the most of them.
4. Target different parts of your neighbourhood with different sets of volunteers.

Community Service

69. Offer to clean up an untidy public space in your local community, in liaison with your local authority.

Christians have sometimes been characterised as 'other-worldly' – focusing on the life to come, disparaging this earthly world and emerging from holy huddles only to preach to 'the lost'. It was an over-exaggeration, but there was a grain of truth in the image. Many modern-day Christians have tried to challenge this perception by presenting a more incarnational model, in which they try to transform society to help everyone. Often this has meant a new focus on Christians serving local communities in practical ways or campaigning for social justice on behalf of others.

This can be seen in the UK in events such as Soul in the City – where young people from Soul Survivor conferences descend en masse on a city to serve residents practically alongside evangelistic events. And the Make Poverty History campaign has seen unprecedented levels of lobbying and campaigning on behalf of the poor in developing countries. It's not that Christians have been uninterested in these issues until recently. It's more that their involvement and methods have now been given a higher profile.

Many individual churches have caught hold of this vision and linked community service and evangelism firmly together. It's good to show that practical love and spiritual salvation come in the same package. Many non-churchgoers are suspicious of being preached at, even by close friends, but most would be impressed by a group going out of their way to offer practical help in menial tasks. Such attitudes are so counter-cultural these days that they will mark out Christians as different.

Cleaning public spaces is one popular way of offering practical service to the community. In most communities, this kind of work is long overdue, high profile and much appreciated – some churches have reported residents coming out of their homes to thank those doing the work for them. It's a good idea to liaise with the local authority as it can direct you to the areas where help is needed most urgently. It's also a good idea to encourage your church's youth group to get involved – many people's perception is that youngsters cause problems with vandalism, graffiti and anti-social behaviour. Your youth group may want to prove that teenagers can be helpful.

How to do it:

1. Liaise with your local authority. Find out where help is needed to clear away rubbish, remove graffiti, cut back weeds or tidy public spaces.
2. Organise a team, ideally consisting mostly of young people, to spend a week or so doing such practical work. You might want to organise an evangelistic event at the end of the week that non-churchgoers can be invited to.

3. Give your team training in how to represent your church effectively: perhaps some advice about what to say if they are approached, or how to publicise your event.
4. Give them t-shirts to wear publicising your event or your church's logo so people know where they are from.
5. Publicise what your teams are doing in the secular media, in your parish magazine if it is delivered around the community, or with specific leaflets that are pushed through people's letterboxes.

Further resources:

For more information on Soul Survivor, see: www. soulsurvivor.com. For more on campaigning to tackle world poverty, see: www.makepovertyhistory.org, www. tradejusticemovement.org or www.christianaid.org.uk

70. Offer practical help to disadvantaged families for free.

Cleaning up public spaces may be effective if you are planning a one-off mission or series of outreach events over a week. You want to do something worthwhile and high profile for a limited period of time. But to gain a longer-term reputation for your church and build specific relationships with individuals, you may want to provide a more personal service. Creating and publicising a scheme in which congregation members offer help to needy families and individuals is one way of doing this. Decorating or other simple DIY jobs, and gardening are two things that are easier to do with a team of willing helpers.

Offering such kindness to complete strangers for free is so counter-cultural that some people are genuinely overwhelmed by it. Their attitude towards their local church may be transformed. They will certainly tell all their friends and family. If this kind of help is offered on a regular basis to those in need, your church should gain the kind of word-of-mouth reputation that money can't buy. This isn't, of course, the only reason to do such things: it should be part of the outworking of our faith to be eager to help in any case.

This can be an arena where men come into their own. That's not to say women can't be involved – far from it. But those men in your congregation, or on the fringes of it, who might find it more difficult to pray or share with a home group about how they are feeling, may feel more comfortable getting stuck into practical tasks.

If your church does establish a team with the time and skills to tackle these kinds of jobs on a regular basis, you could publicise its existence among those professionals who come into contact with needy people: social workers, health visitors, GPs and others. If they discover a family or individual that would appreciate this kind of practical help, they could (with permission) pass on the contact details to the church, which could send a team around. In doing so, you will also enhance the reputation of your congregation in the eyes of such professionals.

How to do it:

1. Recruit a team that is willing to help with practical tasks. Look beyond your immediate congregation, as non-churchgoing husbands of churchgoers and others on the

fringes of your church may be interested in getting involved.

2. Discover the skills that members of your team can offer. Some tasks may require more complex skills, others may not. Decide what kind of practical tasks you can offer.

3. You may want your team to tackle a job on behalf of a church member first to test those skills and decide on the best method of tackling such jobs.

4. Advertise your services, perhaps initially among the congregation. They can then offer your help to their neighbours and friends.

5. If you have the capability to tackle such jobs regularly, offer your services via professionals working in your community. Ensure that the help you offer is of a high standard.

6. Do say 'no' to jobs that are beyond your capabilities. The reputation of your church will not be enhanced if you make a mess of things.

Further resources:

For more information on helping to link those with time, money or resources with those who are needy, contact The Besom, who can put you in touch with local groups already doing this work. See: www.besom.com

71. 'Bless your community' by using church funds to pay for small but significant things that will brighten up people's days.

The idea that churches are constantly involved in fund raising is ingrained in many people's minds. Call at someone's house saying you're from the church and many will automatically assume you want a contribution to some building fund. It's hardly surprising when you consider how many of the UK's listed buildings are churches, and that congregations receive little government help to preserve and maintain that national heritage. But it's unfortunate if the only perception people have of 'church' in your community is of people interested in their wallets. This perception is reinforced by thermometer-style signs outside your building showing how much has been raised, or constant requests for money inside the building.

So for a congregation to be giving money away, or spending it on the local community, can be genuinely surprising. The idea of 'blessing your community' is a relatively recent one in the UK, but has been taken up by several congregations. Typically, it involves giving £100 or so to each of your house groups and allowing them to decide a way of spending the money to brighten up the lives of those in their local community. That might be something as simple as bringing coffee and cakes to those working in your local shops or providing birthday cards for OAPs in your local sheltered housing complex. You might offer to provide 'pampering packs' (nice soaps, perfumes and make-up) for women in a local hostel, or offer to buy appropriate Christmas presents for residents in a local children's home. Ideally it will be something that you can indicate comes from the local church with no strings attached. Once again, your church's reputation will be enhanced.

How to do it:

1. Agree to commit a certain amount of church funds to this kind of project.
2. Think of suitable ways to use the cash. You may want to allow each of your house groups to decide how to spend an amount each. This helps to emphasise that this is a gift from individual church members to individuals in the community.
3. It might be appropriate for house group suggestions to be approved by the church leadership, in case there are ideas that might be inappropriate or insensitive.
4. Publicise in the local media the fact that your church is using its money to 'bless the community'.

72. Throw regular free events as gifts to your community.

The idea of providing a free service to your local community can, of course, be extended into other areas. Churches often use events such as fairs, fun days, plays and concerts to raise money, so to provide such events for free can also challenge people's perceptions. It communicates something important: that you value those in your community so much that you are prepared to entertain them at your own expense. It also changes the whole nature of the event: the driving force behind it can be welcoming people into your church family rather than trying to empty their wallets. Visitors do notice the difference.

Imagine the impact of holding a free family fun day for those in your local community. Your church displays its hospitality and generosity by paying for bouncy castles, face-paints and children's entertainers, and organising games and activities. It gives away fun packs at the end of the day, including balloons emblazoned with your church's logo, and leaflets publicising church activities. Grateful parents and satisfied children go home at the end of the day deeply appreciative of what your church has been able to offer. Lay on enough of this kind of event, and you should discover even the most cynical non-churchgoer admitting that you're not just after their money.

Of course, if your church has traditionally relied on this kind of event to pay for church building repairs or significant building projects, you may think this simply isn't possible. The loss of the income from your summer fair or series of music concerts could put a serious dent in your annual budget. To a certain extent, embracing this kind of concept requires congregations to understand changes in our society. In previous years, non-churchgoers may have been happy to help pay for the upkeep of a church building they felt was a vital part of their local heritage. These days, fewer of them are likely to care. Your congregation needs to know that asking such people to fund your church's upkeep through constant fundraising events will affect its reputation. If fundraising events do need to happen, at least make sure that you lay on some free ones too.

How to do it:

1. Put aside some money for free events. If the cash comes from your 'mission' or 'outreach' budget, your congregation is more likely to approach the event with the right attitude.

2. Publicise the event widely, using posters, your parish magazine, leaflets and the secular media. Make sure the word 'free' features prominently.
3. Make sure the event provides plenty of interesting activities, or a high-quality music or theatrical experience. Provide a good welcome for people.
4. Have information about church activities or welcome packs available for people to take home.

Media Liaison

73. Recruit someone to promote good news about your church.

It's easy to criticise newspapers, magazines, radio and TV stations for misrepresenting Christianity, focusing on church scandals and doctrinal rows. Sometimes worshippers despair of their local and national media reporting some of the good news that they know is happening in their church and others nearby. This is partly because of the inevitable media focus on the extraordinary – 99 ministers behaving themselves is not very interesting; one minister misbehaving obviously is. But this may also be our own fault for not promoting what we do in the secular media well enough.

Past experience can make us wary of contacting the media. Didn't they twist what the pastor said last time? Didn't they ignore our event last year – so surely they won't be interested this time? Aren't they prejudiced against churches anyway? Well, if we all took that view, few outside the church would know any of the good news going on in our churches – yet it wouldn't stop the bad news from getting reported. It's important to 'keep the rumour of God alive' by making sure that good news about Christians is reported, however hamfistedly. And it's simply not true that there is a bias against churches. If it's a good enough story, it will be reported, whatever its source.

But this all needs some planning in advance. Those attending a church event might think: 'This would look really good in our local newspaper.' But by the time it's happening, it's too late to do anything about it. The media normally prefer to know about an event *before* it actually happens – to write a report previewing it rather than reflecting on it afterwards, and to decide whether it is important enough for them to attend.

It's also helpful to think about the kind of stories that the media are interested in. Flick through your nearest newspaper or magazine. It should be obvious that the media tend to be interested in stories about people rather than stories about events. Why? Because we, their readers, are normally more interested in people. We chat in the office about celebrity gossip, not forthcoming events. We listen to sermons more attentively when the preacher tells a story about someone we know, not when they detail abstract doctrine. But discovering and communicating interesting stories about people in your church takes time.

So this area needs some planning. But it would be wrong to leave all the work to your minister. He or she will have enough to do running the church, and will also be called on anyway if the local media want some kind of comment on an issue. Why not recruit someone from your congregation who can contact the media whenever you have good news to promote?

How to do it:

1. Find someone who has the necessary time to devote to media liaison to be 'publicity officer'. It doesn't need to be someone with journalistic skills, but someone who can respond quickly – either to a request from the church leadership for a press release to be sent out or to a response from a reporter. It could, of course, be a professional PR firm, if finance permits.

2. If necessary, give your publicity officer some training in how to write a good press release (see Idea 74) and make sure they have access to the necessary equipment (perhaps a PC, internet access, fax machine and digital camera).

3. Make sure your publicity officer is involved in the planning of church events, or knows what is on the horizon well in advance. If you are trying to promote a church event, make sure he or she has all the correct details (venue, contact numbers, ticket prices) at their fingertips.

4. Make sure that people in your congregation know who your publicity officer is, and publicise their contact details so they can be approached with ideas.

5. Tell your publicity officer details about people within your congregation who have interesting stories of faith to tell.

74. Learn how to write press releases that will be used.

The busy reporter or news editor will see hundreds of press releases or items of information each day that they could make into stories. If you want to promote your church effectively, you have to convince them that your story is more worthwhile than virtually all the others. You will also be competing against a heavy news agenda, ideas generated by the reporter or news editor themselves, and events that are already in their diaries. It's little wonder that information about church activities often ends up at the bottom of their in-tray.

Learning how to write effective press releases involves understanding more about news values. This isn't some secret code that only journalists and PR firms understand – it's common sense, and can be gleaned by a quick look at any publication or broadcast. The most common reason for church press releases not being used by the local or national media is failure to grasp these principles.

News can be any, or a combination, of the following:

(i) *Something new.* If something is ongoing, it's probably not news. But if it's happening for the first time, it might be. Remember that the media like to be first with the news, so emphasise the newness of it. If you have an ongoing building project, emphasise that this is a new phase of the work. So 'New children's service to be launched' is more newsworthy than 'Children's services are happening'.

(ii) *Something out of the ordinary.* If every other church is doing what yours is doing, your event is probably not news. But if you're doing something different – or something normal, but in an extraordinary way – it might be. That's why quirky stories about vicars abseiling from church roofs to raise funds or ministers preaching continuously for 48 hours are used. And, because the secular media often have an outdated idea of what church services are like, it's possible for the most standard of worship services to sound revolutionary simply by emphasising the use of drama, guitars or PowerPoint equipment. So 'Vicar DJs in local nightclub' is more newsworthy than 'Vicar launches church roof appeal'.

(iii) *Something local.* If there is no local link to the story, it's probably not news for the local media. If there is, it might be. Tell the local media about an appeal to help a Christian charity working overseas, and they won't be interested. Tell them that a local person has done something quirky to raise money for it and they may be. So 'Local Baptist church revamps its image' is more newsworthy for the local media than 'Baptist church nationwide revamps its image'.

(iv) *Something about a person, not an event.* A forthcoming meeting is probably not news, but a personal angle on it might be. People stories are always more newsworthy, and we may have lots of interesting people within our congregations, from the youngster travelling abroad on a gap-year to the stalwart who hasn't missed a Sunday service in 50 years. And if you must promote an event, try to do it by focusing on a person involved. So 'Betty organises flower festival for 40th consecutive year' is more newsworthy than 'Flower festival happens'.

(v) *Something visual.* A story that doesn't immediately suggest a photo is probably not news, but something photogenic might be. If you can suggest a possible photo or something that can be filmed, the media will be more interested. If your story is about a minister abseiling off your church roof, the visual element may be obvious. In other cases it may not be, and you may need to suggest something. Study your local TV news or newspaper and examine what kind of things they photograph or film. So 'New website projected onto side of cathedral to celebrate launch' is more newsworthy than 'New cathedral website launched'.

The best stories, of course, combine all these elements, but just one of them could lift it above the mundane. Writing a press release incorporating these elements is not necessarily a difficult thing, so long as some simple rules are followed. You don't have to have journalistic flair or an English degree – just the ability to get the right facts in front of the reporter. They will almost certainly rewrite your offering anyway.

How to do it:

1. Make sure you start preparing your press release well in advance of the event you want to publicise, by gathering all the necessary facts.

2. Study the local media and write down contact details for your local reporters, or the newsdesk involved. Ring the media outlet and ask for the personal e-mail address of the reporter who deals with church matters or your particular part of town. Get the number of the fax machine used by editorial staff.

3. Use your church's headed notepaper so the reporter knows it's authentic.

4. Write down the facts: *who* is involved, *what* is happening, *where* it is happening, *why* it is happening, and so on. Try to put as much information suggesting why this is topical, extraordinary, local, people-centred and visual into the first sentence, as that might be as much as the reporter has time to read.

5. Avoid church jargon. If necessary, explain complex concepts in brackets for the benefit of the reporter. Avoid puns or suggested headlines: they won't be used.

6. Stick to one side of A4 if you can.

7. Include a quote from your minister, or the person involved, as this always livens up a story. Make sure it sounds conversational, not stilted – and check it's OK with the person before you send it.

8. Include contact details for the person the press release is about and your minister, so the reporter can check any further details.

9. Include a chance for a 'photo opportunity' ahead of the

event, and during office hours, if possible. Be flexible and prepared to change this time if it's inconvenient.

10. Copy and paste the text of your press release into the body of an e-mail (reporters usually won't bother to open attachments) and e-mail it to all the reporters who cover your area. Simultaneously fax it to the numbers you gathered earlier.

11. Wait for a response. If none comes within a couple of days, ring up and ask whether the reporter plans to use the press release. If not, don't demand to know why – ask them whether the story is the kind of thing they are interested in and learn from their response.

75. Learn how to give good interviews.

If you're successful in gaining the attention of the local media, or even national media outlets, your publicity officer or minister will be asked to give interviews at some point. Sometimes they might be on a subject of your choice – the event or person you wanted to publicise – but they may be on a topical religious issue or a tricky moral subject. If the media realise that people at your church are not only willing to be interviewed, but are good at it, they are more likely to ask again.

Many people are terrified at the thought that their words might be twisted out of context or used in a way they didn't expect. Of course, it's possible that the reporter has some kind of hidden agenda, but you only learn from experience – which may include making the odd mistake.

And, of course, an interview on the radio or TV may be very different from an interview in a newspaper or magazine. Bear in mind that a live TV or radio interview needs to be more like a conversation that can continue for several minutes. An interview for a newspaper may last just as long, but only a couple of sentences may be used.

How to do it:

1. Find out something about the programme or publication so that you know what your target audience is. A regional TV programme will be different from a national Christian periodical. Target your preparation accordingly.
2. If it is a broadcast interview, find out whether it will be live or pre-recorded, and be aware of the opportunities and dangers either option gives you. A live interview means the broadcaster can't edit what you will say, but it can be an intimidating prospect. A pre-recorded interview means you can stop in mid-flow and ask to start again, but your comments may be edited down to a half-sentence that may not be exactly what you intended to say.
3. Offer the interviewer a background briefing. In a broadcast studio, ask the presenter if anything is unclear before you start. Or ask them what their first question will be. With newspaper reporters, it is OK to suggest that you are speaking 'off the record' to fill in some of the background before you agree on an actual quote. But don't say anything 'off the record' that you would be upset to see in print.
4. If you are rung out of the blue and need time to gather your thoughts, offer to ring the reporter back. Use the time to jot down some bullet points and check your facts if you are unsure about anything, and then ring back within their deadline if it is looming.

5. Much of the impression that you make on TV or radio depends on what you look and sound like. So check you haven't got food in your teeth and that your shirt has been ironed. Once you are being interviewed, smile, and talk slowly – most people who are nervous speak too fast.

6. Listen to the questions and try to answer them. If you have something that you really want to say, by all means say it, but go back to answering the original question. Offer anecdotes or real-life examples to explain what you mean.

7. Avoid church jargon.

8. Don't be intimidated. The chances are that you will know more about the subject than your interviewer. If they say something wildly inaccurate, correct them, but do so gently.

9. In a newspaper interview, ask them to read back to you the quotes they plan to use in the story. It may be that you have to stress that some of things you said are conditional, or that the whole sentence should be used, not just part of it.

10. Be prepared for the difficult or the cynical question. Answer it in a firm but friendly voice, however riled you may feel.

76. Take digital photos of events and e-mail them to media outlets.

Media outlets these days are often overstretched and under-resourced. Journalists are desperately trying to fill more pages, often with fewer staff than before. Anything that you can do to make their job easier will be appreciated.

With the advent of digital cameras, it's never been easier to supply the print media with photos of what's happening in your church. Of course, different publications may have different views about how they use contributed photos – some local newspapers may welcome them, while others may swear they never use them. Much depends on the quality of your photos.

The widespread use of digital cameras, of course, doesn't necessarily guarantee that quality. It may be better to be sparing about sending photos to newspapers. If picture editors know you've always supplied good quality photos in the past, they may be more eager to receive them in future. If you've inundated them with inferior quality photos, they may decline your offers. You can, of course, if finance permits, hire professional photographers to take photos at your events.

How to do it:

1. Inform the local press beforehand about your event. If their own photographer turns up, you may not need to bother taking your own photos.
2. If you end up taking the photos yourself, think about their *content*. The media will only use one photo, so what one image would sum up this event? If it's the launch of your building project, what about the vicar in a hard hat holding a hod of bricks? If it's a family fun event, what about a child wearing colourful face-paints holding a balloon?
3. Photos of people enjoying themselves are always more likely to be used, so don't try taking a photo of a reluctant subject.
4. Get someone to pose for the photo, rather than taking it unawares. That way, you can get exactly what you want.

5. The most common fault in amateur photographs is that the photographer hasn't got close enough to the subject. No picture editor will be interested in a photo that includes huge amounts of sky or grass. Close-ups of people's faces are far more interesting.

6. Jot down some details of the event and e-mail the photo directly to the picture editor and/or the news editor of your local newspaper. Do so that day if you can, even if your local paper is a weekly one. Include contact details so a reporter can find out more, if necessary.

7. Ring the next day to check that your photo has been received. Ask if it is likely to be used. If not, learn from any mistakes you may have made.

77. Speak out on controversial issues, especially if they are on the news agenda.

Some people compare the media to a pack of baying dogs. One day, something will be at the top of the news agenda, and everyone will want an interview or a photograph. The next day, they will have moved on to something else. The 'pack' mentality comes because no one wants to be left behind in covering a particular story. It does mean that it's easy to predict what that day's 'big issue' is likely to be – just check the news at breakfast-time.

If something comes up that your church is particularly interested in, why not take the chance to speak out on that subject? If a new report on homelessness suggests that the problem is increasing nationally, and your church has a local project that is dealing with more and more homeless people, you will make a reporter's life much easier by pointing that connection out. It creates an instant 'local angle' on a national news story. And it reinforces the message that your church is caring for such people. The next time that reporter does a story on the subject, he or she may come to your church for a comment first.

But time is of the essence. If your local newspaper comes out every evening, its deadlines will be throughout the morning. And if you delay contacting your local radio station until the afternoon, the news agenda may already have moved on. It's important that your publicity officer can contact your pastor, minister, community worker or youth worker to clarify exactly what your church wants to say in this situation.

It may also be appropriate for your church to speak out on a controversial local subject. A minister may feel that it is part of his or her remit to serve their community to speak out on – or even lead a media campaign about – issues such as the closure of a rural post office, the lack of local job opportunities or a planning dispute.

Do bear in mind though that it's easy to get sucked into what newspapers call a 'war of words'. If the big issue of the day is abortion and your church gives an anti-abortion line, the reporter will want to balance those comments with quotes from a local abortion clinic or pro-life group. If you haven't taken care over your quotes or checked your facts thoroughly, your church's opinions may be rubbished.

How to do it:

1. Make sure your church's publicity officer has access to national and local newspapers, radio and TV news each morning.

2. Make sure he or she has access to the minister or other church contacts easily in case a relevant subject comes up.

3. Agree a way by which your church will comment: will the publicity officer write down a suggested quote and pass it on to the minister for approval? Or would it be better for the minister to come up with something to say?

4. Make your comments brief: no more than a few sentences. Don't get lost in theology or church jargon, but equally don't make your comments so simplistic that they can be rubbished by those who hold the opposite view.

5. Check any facts you use thoroughly. If possible, use examples from your own church's experience which add weight to the opinion expressed.

6. E-mail and fax your comments to each of your local media.

78. Put a positive spin on bad news.

'Spin' has become a dirty word in media circles. It suggests deception – or at least being economical with the truth – to get the coverage you want. But it needn't involve any of the tricks of media manipulation: sometimes it might just mean salvaging something positive out of a bad news story.

Churches experience bad news stories about scandals, problems or arguments constantly. That's partly because people expect church congregations, and ministers in particular, to have higher moral standards than others. When they slip, and a vicar commits adultery or a congregation is split down the middle on a point of principle, it can easily become news. The media may also side with someone who has suffered a perceived injustice at the hands of your church – perhaps over the siting of a gravestone or the hire of a church hall. The passions invoked when issues of doctrine are discussed usually throw up good quotes too.

The management of bad news stories in many organisations, including the Church, often starts and finishes with a 'no comment'. Inevitably, this can make the Church seem ultra-defensive, as if it has something to hide. Often it doesn't help that the minister may be unable to comment, because if he or she told the real story, it would mean breaking confidences.

But it's possible not only to find something to say, but to use the fact that your church is in the spotlight to say something positive. If your minister upset a couple who were getting married at your church with an ill-advised comment during the sermon, it might be plastered all over the front page of your local paper. Not only could he or she apologise (which suggests a Christian sense of repentance), but your pastor could send the couple a bunch of flowers and agree to pose for photos with the couple and the flowers. The alternative (a 'no comment' and a refusal to talk to the media) won't prevent the ill-advised remarks being reprinted every time your church is mentioned in the media.

How to do it:

1. When contacted about a bad news story, ask the reporter what deadline they are working towards, and promise to call back before that deadline with a comment. Ask the reporter what they know already – perhaps they don't have the full story or completely accurate information.
2. Think about the issue itself. Is it a genuine point of

principle that the church should refuse to budge on? Does the reporter or perhaps the person who complained about the church's attitude need to know more background about how a decision was reached? Or is it something where an apology would help?

3. Write down what you think you should say. In some cases, it may simply be an explanation of why you can't comment, which at least is better than a blanket refusal to talk. Ring back the reporter and read out your comment.

4. You will be asked more questions about the subject. Refuse to say anything other than what you have decided to say – unless something new is brought up. If so, promise to get back to them and repeat the process.

5. Once the initial crisis is over, think of a way of creating a positive spin on the story: if your church has let a member of the public down, could you apologise and present them with a gift? Could you listen to their point of view, even if you don't agree with it? Could you change your church's policy on a particular issue (e.g. child protection or the recruitment of volunteers) that may allay public concern?

6. Contact the reporter who originally spoke to you and tell them what you plan to do. Make sure other media know about it too.

Further resources:

Training courses on all aspects of media liaison are run jointly by all the denominations in the UK Church. See: www.commstraining.org.uk for details. Your local diocese or district may also offer similar training.

Website

79. Create a church website, or revamp
your existing one.

A website is a fantastic resource. It enables you to tell the whole world what your church stands for, gives them an idea of the activities you offer, and even allows people to contact your church leadership directly. It's hardly surprising that many churches have embraced this technology to appeal to those who don't come to church. Many of us now use the internet as our first port of call for information on virtually any subject. So if you don't exist in cyberspace, you're virtually invisible to large sections of the population.

However, in the rush to embrace the new technology, there are three traps that churches often fall into. Here are three questions you might like to ask before you start:

(i) Who is it for?

Churches often commission someone from their congregation – or even a commercial firm – to create a website without thinking who they are trying to reach. But the purpose of your website should dictate its content and style. Only when you know why you are doing it should you think about what to say and how to say it.

Perhaps your church attracts tourists. Then your website might concentrate on its history, artefacts and architecture, but also include details of your activities. Perhaps yours is a large church and you want to use the website to help church members keep in touch with what's happening and with each other. A diary of events, lists of church activities and contact details will be important. You could provide a bulletin board, so church members can talk to each other, or sermon texts, in case they've missed a week. Perhaps your website is designed to be evangelistic. If so, why not make it interactive, as well as including information about your church and its activities? Include features so people can ask questions about your faith or even read helpful verses or prayers online.

(ii) How will people find it?

Many churches seem to be satisfied to have websites that simply exist, as if their mere presence in cyberspace was enough. Of course, if someone specifically looks for the Church of St Botulph's-in-the-Undergrowth, they will find your site. But if your website is designed to be evangelistic, you want web users to be able to 'stumble' across it when they are actually looking for something else entirely.

Modern search engines are so powerful that you don't need to 'register' with any of them. But do mention your town or city on the home page, so it can appear if someone types in the word 'church' and the name of your locality. Look for ways to link with other church and community sites too. If your church is a tourist attraction, make sure there are links from the tourist sites serving your locality. If you do lots of community activities, ask for links from websites run by your local authority, village or community. Make sure there are links from your denomination's national or regional site too.

And do make sure that every single poster, leaflet, newsletter – and even your church leader's headed notepaper – contains a reference to the website where people can find more information. If people see all these references to your website, they may eventually look at it.

(iii) How will it be updated?

It's not enough to create a website and then leave it floating in cyberspace. Items quickly become out of date, and people – including regular churchgoers – will stop visiting it if it hasn't changed after two or three visits. Ideally, your home page should look slightly different each time, and the easiest way to do this is to have some kind of high profile 'Latest News' or 'Forthcoming Events' section at the side of the page.

The question about how it will be updated becomes especially pertinent if you have asked a teenager who is heading off to university or a commercial firm to create the site for you. You don't want to be in a situation where you don't have the password, the software or the expertise to update it. Whoever creates your website should be able to provide you with a simple way to

update pages – ideally in such a way that if you press
the wrong button, you will only affect the content of
one page, rather than deleting the entire website.

These are the kinds of questions you might want to consider
before creating or revamping a church website. You may
also have questions about which internet service provider
(ISP), domain name and software to use. It's difficult to rec-
ommend specific ISPs, as their offers will change over time;
do shop around to see which gives you the best deal. Try to
use a memorable domain name (e.g. www.stmarysany
town.org.uk rather than one based on the name of the ISP
such as www.[name of ISP].co.uk/freespace/stmarysany
town, which is harder to remember).

The type of software people prefer is incredibly subjec-
tive: it tends to reflect what they are already used to. If you
have asked a congregation member to create a church website, and he or she recommends software that can be easily
used by your church's leadership or parish administrator to
update pages, that's probably fine. A commercial firm will
probably use a more complex type of software, but as long
as it is easy for you to update pages, that's fine too.

The content of your site will be dictated by its purpose. If
you are creating a site for the first time, its initial content
may be relatively basic: make sure you provide people with
details of where your church is, when your services take
place, what style of worship is offered, an idea of the range
of activities on offer, and some contact details. As the site
develops, more content specific to the purpose of your site
may be added.

The design of your website is also important. Website

design is slightly different from the design of a book or magazine. You do need an overall 'look' to each page, perhaps with your church's logo in the top left-hand corner and your church's name across the top of each page (people may access any of your pages without starting at the home page). Do try to use pictures to show what your church activities or services look like. But they don't need to be large – 72dpi and 'thumbnail' size is usually adequate. And use a simple font for text consistently throughout.

Many websites these days use what is called a dynamic content management system. This means web designers don't design every single page. They might design a consistent background and layout; and pieces of text are stored in various databases. When the web user asks for a certain page to be displayed, the page will consist of a design taken from one place and some text taken from elsewhere. You

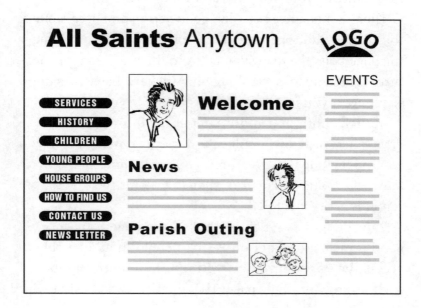

don't need to understand exactly how this works, except that it means your website can be a lot more flexible.

There is a balance between good design and accessibility: the fussier the design or the larger the photos, the longer the page will take to download. And the more complex features (video images, scrolling news tickers, flash animation sequences) you include, the less accessible your site will be. Although more and more people have broadband these days, such pages will still take time to download. If you want to include those features, you could limit them to certain pages, and make sure that the majority of your site remains accessible to all.

Your design also includes links from page to page. One good principle to work on is that people should be able to access the page they want with the minimum number of clicks from your home page. That might mean a main menu on the home page, and each of those main menu options leads to pages where more detailed options are available.

How to do it:

1. Think about why you would like to create a website, or why you have one at the moment. How will that affect its content and design?
2. Ask either someone from your congregation or a commercial firm to design or redesign a site for you. Brief them on the purpose of the site, discuss how the site might be updated and provide them with the text, photos and any church logos they need. Discuss also the issue of accessibility.
3. Whoever is creating your site, ask them to draw a site map for you so you can see how easy it is for web users to get from the home page to the pages they want. If necessary, change the menu lists to prioritise certain pages over others.
4. Register a suitable domain name and include your web address on all items of church literature.
5. Go online and discover which other organisations in your locality have websites. Ask for links to be created to your church's site. If your village or community has a well-visited, well-designed and constantly updated website, it might even make more sense to ask if one of its pages might be devoted to your church, rather than creating a site of your own that might be little used.
6. Discuss who will update your site, and how often. Is it something your parish administrator could do? Or, if the person who created your website is part of your congregation, could they do so?

7. Keep reviewing the statistics of how many visitors your website has and which pages are visited most often. Keep reviewing the content and design of your site in the light of these statistics.

Further resources:

Training courses on the creation of websites are run jointly by all the denominations in the UK Church. See: www.commstraining.org.uk for details. Your local diocese or district may also offer similar training.

80. Allow people to subscribe to a regular e-newsletter telling them what's happening at your church.

Some people might not look twice at items of written church literature, but check their e-mails constantly. It can therefore help to have some kind of e-newsletter that can be sent out to church members or others who are interested. That doesn't mean someone needs to spend a long time creating a unique web publication. But information that is already communicated in other ways – church newsletters, leaflets, verbal notices and the weekly leaflet – can also be sent out via e-mail. This might be a monthly e-newsletter, but the beauty of e-mail is that you can actually send out information about an event as soon as it's ready, without waiting for a publication deadline. You can also send out updates about what new things have been added to your church's website.

Most congregation members would be happy enough to

give the church's office or leadership their e-mail addresses, so that creates a ready-made distribution list. But you may want to include a feature on your website that allows people to register for regular e-newsletters. You may discover that information about your events and activities is therefore sent around the world, as well as to locals.

Once you have such a distribution list, you must be careful not to abuse it. If you send out huge e-mails with lots of photos, graphics or other attachments, you won't be enhancing your church's reputation. In fact, your e-newsletters don't need to include any graphics, photos or HTML coding at all. A few lines of plain text on each item, perhaps with a link to the relevant page on your website, will suffice.

How to do it:

1. Collect e-mail addresses from congregation members, explaining why you would like to do so. Create a distribution list of those who are happy to be contacted in this way.
2. Add a feature to your website allowing people to register for regular e-newsletters. This could simply be by sending an e-mail to the parish office or church webmaster. Add their e-mail addresses to your distribution list.
3. Summarise information from existing pieces of church literature in brief paragraphs, with links to the relevant page on your website, if appropriate. Add details about new pages or features on your website.
4. Send out these e-newsletters regularly. Don't overdo it,

as sending out the same information all the time will soon start to grate.

81. Create a bulletin board on your website to give people a reason to return to your site.

It's important to create reasons for people to visit your website – and to return frequently. That way, they'll see the latest information about your events and activities. One way that seems to work is to have a bulletin board, which allows the web user to interact with others online. If someone has contributed to a debate, they are much more likely to go back to that site to see what others have said in response.

There's usually a lot to debate in church life – we expend a lot of energy talking about styles of worship, theology, social issues and so on. So this should be a fruitful arena to add to our church website. You'll need to decide first what kind of debate you would like to have. A completely free, open debate for anyone who logs on is one possibility. The advantage of this is that no one feels excluded and queries from non-churchgoers can be answered easily, but church members may not feel happy debating particular worship styles if they feel non-regulars are reading their criticisms. You might also need to create a secure, password protected part of the website, as well as or instead of a public forum.

How to do it:

1. Investigate online firms that can provide you with a bulletin board for your website. Some will charge a fee,

some may ask you to accept some advertising, so it's important to find the right one. Your Internet Service Provider may be able to help.

2. Create some different 'discussion threads' (i.e. subjects for discussion), perhaps by starting off with some questions designed to stimulate debate.

3. Publicise the fact that the bulletin board is there – perhaps with an e-mail bulletin to those who have subscribed to receive them from your church.

4. Monitor people's contributions. You may need to remove inappropriate messages.

5. Start new discussion threads as appropriate. Try to make them topical, perhaps by focusing on a particular national issue, or something that is happening in your local community.

82. Put spiritual resources on your website so web users can engage with their spirituality at home.

The flourishing of the internet does give the Church unprecedented opportunities to help web users engage with their spirituality online. The web isn't there just to provide cold, hard facts. It can actually help people to pray as they sit at their computer screens. There are Christian websites where you can say a prayer and light a virtual candle without leaving your armchair. There are virtual churches that are entirely web-based – members never meet each other or engage in worship together except when they are online.

Your church's website can help some people engage with their spirituality in a more modest way. You could add prayers, perhaps your denomination's 'set prayer' of the day, prayers about current world issues, a Bible verse or a 'Thought for the Day' each day (a dynamic content management system could make this happen automatically).

People often search the internet for prayers and worship resources after a major national or international tragedy. If you can post some suitable prayers on your church's website relatively quickly after such an event, you may discover that they are being used all around the world.

How to do it:

1. Think about the kind of prayers that web users might be searching for – prayers to say after bereavement, healing prayers or prayers of comfort for the lonely or anxious. Or think of Bible verses or spiritual 'thoughts' that would be helpful.
2. Add some of these items to your website. If you are using a dynamic content management system, create a function so your prayers, Bible verses or 'thoughts' change each day or week.
3. If there is some kind of national or international tragedy, and your church has created some liturgy, prayers or worship ideas for a service or school assembly, do add them to your website so others can use them. Create a link from your home page to them.

Further resources:

Examine online churches such as the Church of Fools at www.ship-of-fools.com or i-church, an online Christian community, at www.i-church.com for ideas about engaging with people's spirituality online.

83. Offer to pray for people's individual needs.

Another way of engaging with people's spirituality online is to allow them to be interactive with prayer requests. Why not include a feature on your website that allows users to ask for prayer, by filling in a form that includes their name, e-mail address and prayer request? Many people appreciate prayer, but don't feel comfortable approaching a church in person. They may feel happy to do so via a website, given the relative anonymity of the internet. These requests could range from the relatively trivial to the heart-rendingly tragic, but if someone has bothered to e-mail a request, it is clearly important to them.

If you create such a feature, you should make sure these requests are prayed for. You might have a prayer group that can do this, or a midweek service in which people can be prayed for by name (not their full name, just in case the requests are confidential). It's probably not appropriate to mention such prayer requests in a main Sunday service, when there is often already a long list of intercessions.

You may want to let the person know that they were prayed for on a certain date. If their request betrays some deeper need – perhaps they have been bereaved, are lonely or depressed, or even have been abused – then you should gently suggest a pastoral visit or the name of an agency that could help them. If they live locally, someone from your church could visit, but if they don't, you may need to get in touch with a colleague in another part of the country or the other side of the world. Even if the initial prayer request doesn't lead to a face-to-face visit from a Christian, the fact that you have taken their request seriously shows that your church cares.

How to do it:

1. Decide how you might handle such prayer requests. Is there a prayer group that already exists, or a midweek service when such prayers could be said?
2. Add a prayer request function to your website. This should be by way of an online form that they fill in with their name, e-mail address and prayer request, before submitting it. It's a good principle not to display some-one's actual e-mail address on a website, as that will encourage spam (unwanted e-mail). Software to help you create such online forms is available to download online.
3. Make sure the requests are prayed for.
4. If appropriate, follow up the prayer request. Discover where the person lives and try to arrange for someone to visit, if appropriate.

Further resources:

To see an online prayer request form, visit the 'spirituality' section of the Anglican Diocese of Portsmouth website, at: www.portsmouth.anglican.org

84. Create car stickers advertising your church's website address.

One good way to spread the word about your website is to create some car stickers featuring the web address. If you give them out to congregation members to stick on the back of their cars, the chances are that other drivers will see them as they sit in traffic queues. The car stickers will also identify the drivers as members of your church, which will also increase your church's profile.

But, just as Christians who display fish symbols on their cars have to be sure they drive courteously, so those drivers displaying your church's website also need to make sure they don't bring shame on your church by hogging the road, speeding or exhibiting road rage.

How to do it:

1. Ask a professional firm to produce some car stickers for you. They should feature your website address, as well as your church logo.
2. Distribute them to congregation members.
3. As an incentive, you could offer a prize to the first car that you see displaying a sticker. Entrants should check the website to see if their car has won.

85. Look at web-streaming of digital video images showing church activities or services on your website.

Imagine the idea of people across the world being able to access video images of your church's activities. New technology and increasing broadband access is making this easier. 'Web-streaming' is the name given to the process by which part of a video is played to an internet user while the rest of the video is being downloaded – which is obviously quicker than waiting for the whole video to be downloaded.

Video images should be even more effective than photos at showing what your church activities are like. You may also be surprised at how many people can access them – many computers these days come with the appropriate software to play video, and other free software is easily available via the web.

Initially, you may want to include only a few minutes of video from one or more of your church activities on your website. But if you already use video in your church services, it might be worth looking at the streaming of whole services as they happen via the web. It would mean people could join in your church's worship from the other side of the world.

A simpler way of promoting interactivity might be to record sermons and allow people to access them via audio files placed on your website. A further innovation is the idea of 'pod-casting' – you allow audio files of sermons or whole services to be downloaded onto portable music players such as i-Pods for people to listen to on the move. Both of these are probably easier and cheaper than web-streaming. But do make sure these kinds of services are offered for free.

How to do it:

1. You will obviously need to be able to video church activities or worship services. Because the process of streaming

reduces the quality of the images anyway, a cheap video camera will be adequate. If you are buying one from scratch, choose a digital video camera rather than an analogue one. Other equipment that you may need includes lights, a tripod and a microphone. And, to transfer the images to your website, you may also need a capture card, connector, streaming server and the relevant software to encode the audio and video files. Some of this software is available free via the web.

2. Ask for some training in web-streaming for those involved in this project. Local colleges may be able to offer this.

3. Film and edit short snippets from various church activities. Link the various snippets together with brief face-to-face interviews or voiceovers in which church members describe what they get out of the activities.

4. Practise with the editing software to create short films to use in church before placing any on the web. Choose the most interesting or exciting snippets for your website that illustrate your church's dynamic nature.

5. Upload them to your website. Provide links to the appropriate software that will help people to view the video images.

Sport

86. Create a church sports team to play in a local league.

Men, in particular, can feel awkward or uncomfortable in some social situations. They can feel even worse at church, where there may be unwritten rules they don't know. Watch men at baptisms or weddings, and they'll be nervously fingering their collars and wondering who to talk to. But put the same men in social situations they are used to – playing in a football team, for instance – and things may be very different. Not only might they take pride in getting to know their team-mates, but they may take the lead in encouraging and exhorting others to do better.

Many churches have discovered that sports teams are good places to create relationships between those who come to church and those who don't. This applies to both men and women, of course. Taking sport seriously suggests that being a Christian doesn't mean you lose your passion for other things. Creating a church team, entering a local league and then inviting non-churchgoers to join your team is a way of being inclusive. Those non-regulars may include the spouses, children, work colleagues and neighbours of those who do go to church. Many of them would love to play in a regular team, and it's much easier to ask someone to contribute their goalkeeping or fast-bowling expertise to your team than to ask them to come to a church service.

But you are actually asking them to join a mini-Christian community. If your team has a strong Christian element, that should show itself in the way team-mates encourage those who are less skilled, and how they approach the opposition. Although your team will take the competition seriously, the principle of 'fair play' – everyone having a turn – should be established early on. Sometimes the first thing people notice about a church team is the lack of swearing or bad tackling on the pitch. It's a subtle way of communicating Christian values. And, because 'belonging' to a Christian community tends to come before 'believing', it's a way of helping non-regulars to feel they belong. Saying a quick prayer together before taking to the pitch might be helpful in some situations, but needn't happen every time.

If your church can offer sports training to children or young people, that will also be valued. When youngsters are old enough to decide for themselves about whether they go to church, some decide not to. This may be a way of keeping them involved in church life.

And if your church manages to produce several sports teams playing in different local leagues, you could hold an annual award-giving ceremony over breakfast or dinner. This could mean each team captain giving a brief résumé of their season and presenting prizes. To emphasise your church's philosophy, the prizes could be for the 'most improved' player in each sport, rather than the best. This may be the one occasion in the year when you might ask a team captain to talk directly about their faith in relation to their sport. Hopefully, by this time, relationships within teams should be well enough established for this not to seem embarrassing.

This kind of thinking could be applied to other activities, including taking part in pub quizzes, going on nature rambles or amateur dramatics. All involve building up relationships by taking part in some activity of mutual interest. All should involve non-regulars learning about what it's like to be part of a Christian community by seeing churchgoers interact with each other in a non-threatening setting.

How to do it:

1. Chat to people within your church. What kind of sport do people play already, or what would they like to play?
2. Investigate local sports leagues. Find out when you could enter a football, rugby or cricket team into the league and what the requirements would be.
3. Get together those who are interested in that sport for some training. This may help you to know what gaps still exist in your team.
4. Ask those within your church to tell relatives, workmates and neighbours that you are looking for players to join the team, and to invite them to join your training.
5. Create a 'squad' of players who can form your team. Check people's availability and make sure you have enough players for each fixture. Try to give everyone a fair chance to take part, whatever their ability.

6. If necessary, talk to the churchgoers in your team, to emphasise that they should treat the opposition with respect, encourage their team-mates, and avoid swearing and unfair tackling.

7. Build up relationships within the team. Once the season is finished, you may want to organise an end-of-season dinner for your team, or a 'sports awards' ceremony. At this point, it would probably be OK to give out information about Alpha courses or ask someone to give a ten-minute speech about their faith.

8. Tell the local media about the progress of your team and the names of the recipients of any awards.

87. Hold a sports day for local families.

An extension of your church's involvement in sport could be an annual sports day for families, perhaps in your church grounds. Again, it's an unthreatening thing to invite people to, especially if it is publicised as a 'family sports day'. Mums and dads should be happy to bring their children to take part in a day of fun races and sports competitions. There may be few other locations or institutions offering these kinds of activities in your area. The parents themselves may also be persuaded to take part with others of their age group.

In the summer, this could include tennis, athletics, rounders and five-a-side football. In the winter, you might be able to offer badminton, table-tennis and volleyball. Or you could hold an event in your local sports centre and include swimming races too.

How to do it:

1. Consider whether any other local institutions, such as schools or your local sports centre, already offer sports days or family activities. This may affect the type of sports you choose to offer.

2. Decide what sports you can lay on inside your church building or hall, or inside your church grounds. If that proves to be difficult, could you hire out your local sports centre for the day?

3. Decide on a programme for the day. Publicise it among church members and within the community.

Further resources:

For more information about using sport as a method of outreach, contact Christians in Sport, or see: www.christians insport.org.uk

Text Messaging

88. Create a regular text message update that can be sent to those with mobile phones.

Text messaging is becoming the primary way that some people keep in touch with friends and family. It's cheaper than a mobile phone call, but can still reach people wherever they are. Text messaging can be more effective than e-mailing, as people check their mobiles more often than their PCs. And, in certain more deprived areas, people are more likely to own a mobile than a computer.

It might seem fanciful to suggest that information from church is so important that you need to be able to send text messages to keep people in touch. But if you've already communicated something about a particular event in various other ways, a text message reminding congregation members that it's happening soon might be helpful. Plenty of people carry electronic diaries as part of their mobiles, so this can be a quick way of getting the information into those diaries.

You can create different lists of mobile numbers to receive different types of text message. One could be for those who want to know details of events. Another could consist of church members to whom you might circulate prayer requests. Such distribution lists could be collated by your parish administrator or prayer co-ordinator respectively, who could then circulate the appropriate messages at the appropriate times.

How to do it:

1. Decide where there is a demand in your church for instant information: for prayer requests or details of events.
2. Collect the mobile phone numbers of those in your congregation who would like to sign up for this service. Do tell them the reason why you would like to do so, and reassure them that they won't be bombarded with 'junk' text messages. You can do this by asking people to text a message to a certain mobile phone.
3. Collect those mobile numbers on the mobile phone used by the parish office or prayer co-ordinator, or collect them on a PC that has the facilities to send text messages to mobile phones. Group those numbers together.
4. Give the relevant person the authority to send out messages as appropriate.
5. Monitor the feedback on this facility. Do people find it helpful, or is it giving them information they already know?
6. Offer the service to others in the community, as appropriate. Would newcomers like to sign up to your text messaging service? Would tourists or overseas students like to do so for a limited period while they are in your neighbourhood? What about those who are interested

in specific events, such as music concerts or youth activities?

89. Make sure your youth leaders know the mobile numbers of all the teenagers in your church.

A mobile phone seems to be incredibly important to a teenager's sense of identity. Rarely will a self-respecting member of your youth group be seen without one. That does make it fairly easy for church youth leaders to contact those in their care. In fact, it's probably almost impossible for the leaders of a church youth group to do the job without using their mobiles.

The advantage of mobiles is that people can be contacted instantly. The disadvantage is that those people are less likely to make firm arrangements to get together at specific times. Most will simply promise to 'ring/text you when I get there'. This seems to apply to teenagers more than most. Giving your youth group a carefully worked out timetable every week from now until next Christmas is a good idea. But if there's going to be any change from the normal schedule, it's probably vital to text them to remind them where they should be and at what time beforehand.

Of course, communication should be two-way: teenagers should be encouraged to ring and text their youth leaders if they need advice or support. There are understandable concerns about youngsters being 'groomed' by mobile phone, so you'll need to make sure that normal child protection procedures apply here.

How to do it:

1. Make sure your youth leader knows how to group mobile phone numbers on his or her mobile so that he or she can send messages to all in the youth group.
2. Encourage them to use the facility to send updates about church activities, prayer requests and any changes to arrangements.
3. Encourage them to be available to respond to requests from teenagers as necessary.

Tourism

90. Make sure your church is represented in tourist information centres.

When you're on holiday, which places do you visit to discover more about that place's history? The local church will often be high on your list. An estimated 20–30 million people visit churches around Britain each year, so the chances are that someone might want to visit yours, however isolated or ugly you might think it is.

And where do people discover which churches to visit? Often it's the local tourist information centre. Why not see if you can produce a brochure extolling the virtues of a visit to your church? Or join other churches to produce a joint brochure, perhaps creating a 'tourist trail' around your locality that they can follow?

Or what about adding details of your church to tourist brochures produced by local authorities? It's possible that those who produce tourist brochures for your area don't know some of the hidden treasures inside your church or churchyard – the important stained-glass window or the gravestone of a high-profile former resident. The advantage of this is that local authorities are likely to circulate their brochures much more widely than you can.

How to do it:

1. Check your local tourist information centres. What information do they already hold about your church? Is it correct and up to date?
2. If they have no information about your church, persuade your church leadership to fund the production of a simple brochure, including a brief history of the church and reasons for visiting it. Include photos and make sure it is professionally printed.
3. Distribute such brochures to local tourist information centres, bed and breakfasts, youth hostels and hotels.
4. If your church is already featured in a brochure, but the information is wrong or out of date, contact the local authority or tourism body responsible, and make sure they receive the correct information.
5. If you are promoting your church as a tourism destination, you may need to make a decision about when to keep the church building open for visitors (see Idea 11).

91. Make information about the history of your church available inside the building.

If you manage successfully to market your church as a tourist destination, it's important that you provide information within your church building to help people understand more about the history of both the building and the congregation. Many churches already do this very well. But in some churches the information may have been produced years ago and now looks tatty or outdated.

One way is to produce a guide book that people can use as they work their way around the church. It can say when and how each part of the church was built and highlight items of particular interest. There's nothing wrong with including some details about current church life in such guide books too – so long as it won't get out of date too quickly. Ideally, such guides should be professionally printed, with photos of each window, artefact or architectural feature of interest, as well as current activities. Churches often ask for payment for such guides, which is understandable. But if you want to emphasise the fact that your church is not interested in people's money, you can make them available for free.

Another way is to produce audio guides – recordings on tape or CD that the visitor can listen to individually as they make their way around the building. Or perhaps you might want to place individual plaques next to each item of interest, so that visitors can read them as they go round. Some churches of particular historical interest also produce postcards, greetings cards and even small booklets to remind visitors of their visit.

If your church is open for tourists and others to visit, you might also want to make spiritual information available for them too. If they feel valued as visitors, they may also choose to pray, talk to church members who are in the building, take away a welcome pack, or even tell family and friends who live nearby to visit too.

How to do it:

1. Check what resources you have in your church building to help tourists.
2. If necessary, collate information you might have already into one guide book or audio guide. If you can, get it professionally printed, including photos of items of interest. Include details about current church life.
3. Put your guides in a prominent position at the entrance to the church.
4. If appropriate, record an audio guide onto CD or tape. You will need to provide several personal cassette or CD players near your door, with headphones, for visitors to use. For security reasons, this may only be appropriate if there are people in your church building at all times.
5. Combine your provision for tourists' information needs with provision for their spiritual needs (see Ideas 19–20).

92. Hold regular open days so people can discover more about the history or ecology of your church.

Perhaps your church is of particular significant historical interest. It might have been built in Saxon or medieval times, or perhaps was a significant Victorian or Edwardian addition to your town's skyline. Perhaps it has an important artefact or gravestone, or possibly the church building had a significant role in a historic event in your locality. That might be something you can take advantage of by holding an open day focusing on the era in which it was built, the artefact or the event in question.

If your church was built in medieval times, why not hold a medieval day, when churchgoers can dress in the relevant costumes, demonstrate medieval pastimes and invite people to look at displays explaining how the church came to be built? If your church was important for harbouring combatants during the Civil War, why not re-create the event by rehearsing and performing a short piece of drama explaining what happened? Or perhaps you might want to hold an open day in which experts demonstrate a wide range of church-related activities through the ages – stone-masonry, bell-ringing, calligraphy, organ-playing or singing?

Another way to promote your church might be to hold an ecology open day. Churches with churchyards host a huge range of plants, flowers, wildlife and insects. If you have an ecological expert in the church, or if there is one in your local community, he or she may be happy to host a day in which families discover more about these things. Local families may find such a day appealing.

However you attract people to your church for an open day, it's always a good opportunity to cater for their spiritual needs as well. Make sure you have welcome packs, displays about church activities and so on available during the day. It also helps people who may consider coming to your church in future to have crossed the threshold already.

How to do it:

1. Consider your church's history. Is it possible to base an open day on the circumstances surrounding its creation or an important event in its history?

2. Recruit people from your congregation who are prepared

to investigate its history and who could organise an open day based on their discoveries. This might also involve research into the activities and costumes of that period. Perhaps you could liaise with a local historical society or civic society that might be prepared to share their expertise or involve their members in the day.

3. Organise and publicise an open day. Make sure families know about it if there are going to be special activities for children.

4. Ask an ecological expert to look in your churchyard. Are there enough examples of interesting flowers, plants or wildlife to make an ecological open day viable?

5. If so, consider whether to end such a day with a service of thanksgiving for God's creation, to link the ecological and the spiritual.

93. Promote your redeveloped church building as an ideal conference or retreat location.

If you have recently redeveloped your church building, you may have some modern, flexible meeting rooms as well as a revamped worship area. You may also want to recoup some of the money you have spent on this. You can promote your building as the ideal place for conferences and retreats, both secular and spiritual. Your church should certainly be cheaper than a hotel, even if it can't offer exactly the same facilities.

To compete with other conference centres or retreat centres already on the market, you may need to provide additional facilities such as refreshments. You will also need to publicise its existence. It might be good to do so in the local area initially, perhaps publicising it as a conference centre for local firms and businesses, many of which may choose to meet away from the office for a training day.

You can also promote your church as a retreat centre. This also means providing accommodation, which may be trickier. But if your church is already a popular place to visit, it might be worth investigating whether you can link up with a local hotel or bed-and-breakfast. If you can create a weekend of spiritual refreshment with some talks and some time for people to reflect and try spiritual exercises, you may be surprised by how popular it proves.

How to do it:

1. Investigate whether there are other conference centres in your area. Ask local firms where they might go for a training day or conference. Look at the prices charged by such locations and investigate whether your church could offer a better deal.
2. Put together a professional-looking brochure extolling the virtues of your building as a conference centre. Include photos and details of facilities available.
3. Distribute your brochure to local firms.
4. Make sure you get some feedback about your facilities. You may need to adjust what you can offer or your prices in the light of that feedback.
5. Investigate whether there are other retreat centres in your area. See what they are offering. Investigate whether you could offer a retreat weekend that provides something different.
6. Liaise with local hotels or bed-and-breakfasts to see if

you could work together to provide accommodation alongside your retreat weekend.

7. Publicise your retreats, perhaps locally at first, to gauge reaction. Review the programme and/or accommodation as necessary.

Further resources:

For more details about how to promote churches as tourist destinations, see: www.churchestourismassociation.info

Miscellaneous

94. Keep a database of those on the 'fringe' with whom your church has had contact.

Many of us are careful when filling out forms, buying items over the internet or giving details to commercial firms. If we're not, our contact details can be passed to third parties who might pester us with unsolicited mail. It would be a bad move for churches to get into such direct mailing strategies, but it shows just how valuable databases of names, addresses, phone numbers and e-mail addresses actually are. It might be a good idea for churches to become more organised about the contact details they do hold about people, especially those on the fringes of church activities. If information sent to such people is carefully targeted, it should then be seen as helpful, rather than 'junk'.

If you have a thriving parent and toddler group at your church, those parents may also be interested in your family services, Sunday school and holiday club. The leaders of your parent and toddler group may do their best to publicise them, but it's helpful every so often to send details of special events or activities to all those families registered.

Such a database can become a powerful tool to help you

communicate. It should include how individuals have come into contact with the church (Alpha course, sports club, baptism enquiry etc.), details of any children, previous churches attended and so on. That will enable those who use the database to know who to target with which information.

Data protection legislation means you need to have people's permission to hold and use their details in this way. It should be made clear why you would like to hold those details and what they will be used for, and people need to be able to opt out of the database. Using a standard form for all church activities might help in this.

How to do it:

1. Find an effective piece of software to help you create a database that can identify different lists of people in different categories. Microsoft Access is one option.

2. Decide who will create and update this database: perhaps your parish administrator, pastoral co-ordinator or the minister.

3. Create standard forms including spaces for people's contact details, information about their families, whether they are also members of other churches and what kind of events they would be interested in hearing about. Include a tick box allowing them to opt out of your mailing system.

4. Ensure these forms are available for the leaders of church activities to use at the appropriate time. In some groups, registration might be appropriate the first time someone attends. Other groups may prefer to be as

unthreatening as possible, only asking people to fill out forms if someone is already regularly attending.

5. Make sure there are forms at the back of church for mid-week visitors and newcomers to Sunday worship to fill in. Ensure your welcome team know about them.

6. Use the database intelligently to ensure people know details about the activities they might be interested in, either by post or e-mail. Ensure there is a facility for people to opt out of your mailings if they would like to, and make sure you respect that decision.

95. Deliver leaflets to people's homes offering to pray for their needs.

Many churches are committed to praying for their locality, often interceding within church services for individual streets, institutions and organisations. Others may pray privately, or in smaller groups, about the specific needs of individuals whom they know. People living in those neighbourhoods probably don't know that this happens.

It's a strange feature of our cultural landscape that people may be incredibly cynical about organised religion, apathetic about churchgoing or sceptical about the value of prayer. But if they are going through hard times and someone offers to pray for them, they can be deeply appreciative. They are grateful for the care shown, almost regardless of whether they feel the prayer has been answered.

One way of engaging with your local community might be to let the residents of a particular street know that you are praying for them. You can ask those residents if they have any specific issues they would like prayed about in confidence by delivering leaflets to households in the relevant streets. The fact that you are prepared to pray for general and specific needs should help your congregation gain a reputation as people who care. And the pastoral team or the minister of your church can follow up that visit on a later date.

How to do it:

1. If you don't have a scheme by which your church prays for each of its streets during Sunday services, consider doing so. It helps congregation members to focus on your locality street by street.
2. Examine the ways in which people could pray for individuals' needs in confidence. What about allocating specific house groups or Bible study groups to pray for the streets in their immediate locality? Or what about a specific slot during a regular prayer meeting?
3. Create some leaflets that let residents know you will be praying for their street next Sunday. Include your church's logo, brief details of Sunday services and contact details. Invite people to ring a particular phone number with any specific prayer requests, but emphasise that those prayers will be said in private.
4. Deliver those leaflets to the households in the relevant street each week. If appropriate, your pastoral team could also knock on people's doors to deliver the leaflets face to face, and even offer to pray for people's needs there and then.
5. Make sure your church does pray for those needs.
6. If appropriate, your minister or pastoral team might want to follow up those visits or phone calls. Those

follow-up visits should be done sensitively, though. A wife might ask for prayer for the state of her marriage without necessarily telling her husband, for instance.

96. Apply for a stand at your local psychic fair to promote Christianity.

Another feature of postmodern culture is that many people who reject organised religion are often happy to embrace a pick-and-mix approach to 'spirituality'. They might believe in the power of crystals, tarot cards, astrology or mediums, without necessarily linking those beliefs together in a coherent philosophy. The good news for Christians is that there are many out there who are genuinely spiritually curious. The bad news is that they often don't think of church as the place to engage with their spirituality.

Perhaps the church should market itself better as a genuinely supernatural religion to attract these kinds of people? We're often so keen to present ourselves as normal, friendly people that we forget that the spiritually curious are often looking for something more mysterious or other-worldly. If your church took out an anonymous advert in the local newspaper, offering a weekend in which people could 'explore their spirituality' in a mystery venue, the chances are that many would sign up. What they would think when they found themselves in their local church is anyone's guess!

The spiritually curious can often be found at events such as psychic fairs, consulting fortune-tellers, mediums and stargazers. If Christians want to appeal to those interested in spirituality, perhaps they should also be there. But is there a danger in presenting Christianity as just one spiritual option among many? And might Christians be opening themselves up to occult forces by placing themselves within what some might think is a spiritually hostile environment? The answer to that depends on how your church feels about the spiritual battle. But it certainly seems better to have Christian spirituality as at least one option among many non-Christian options.

How to do it:

1. Discover when and where the psychic fairs in your locality are taking place, by looking at adverts in the local press.
2. You may want to do some reconnaissance, by visiting one of them to see how it operates. This may give you an idea about whether most stalls seem spiritually dangerous or just harmless superstition. Discuss the idea with your church leadership.
3. If you decide to go ahead, contact the organisers and explain what you can offer. Be clear about exactly what you will do – perhaps give out leaflets, pray for the sick or offer counselling.
4. Recruit a team to look after the stall, ideally of spiritually mature, experienced Christians. Give them training in praying for healing, in counselling and apologetics so they know exactly what is expected of them.
5. If appropriate, recruit a separate team to pray for them during the fair. You may also want to explain the thinking behind the idea to your congregation to allay any fears.

6. Make sure your team takes information about your church into the fair to give away.

7. Evaluate the effectiveness of getting involved, to decide whether you should do so again.

97. Take out a pitch at your local car boot sale, wedding fair or secular village fete to publicise church activities.

Many who don't go to church on Sundays choose to go to car boot sales instead – paying good money to buy second-hand items direct from their owners. It's the kind of place where the church needs to be visible. It's obviously important for most of your congregation to be in church on Sundays, but there's nothing wrong with asking a few to take turns running a stall at your local car boot sale.

The same is true of wedding fairs. Bizarrely, even though many couples prefer church weddings, there's often no church representation at wedding fairs. Everyone else is there: photographers, bridal dressmakers, flower arrangers and so on. Why not take a stand there and invite people to consider having a church wedding? And village fetes also provide an ideal opportunity to promote activities at your local church.

How to do it:

1. Discover when and where car boot sales, wedding fairs and village fetes are happening locally. This might involve attending some of these events and picking up information about the next one.

2. Talk to the organisers about taking a stand. You may
   need to pay for this. Explain what you plan to give away.

3. Recruit a team of people to look after your stand. It's good
   if they are people who know all about your church's activities and are good at engaging strangers in conversation.

4. Supply your team with welcome packs or leaflets about
   church activities. If you plan to take a stand at a wedding
   fair, it would be helpful to have a leaflet outlining your
   church's policy on weddings, particularly the remarriage
   of divorcees.

5. If the event is a weekly one, such as a car boot sale,
   organise a rota of people to look after your stand.

98. Give out invitations welcoming people to come back to church.

It might surprise those of us who spend much of our lives
devising ways to get people into church, but there are many
in our communities who would love to be invited. Often
they are older people who went to church as children,
stopped going for some reason, and now feel that coming
back would somehow mark them out as hypocrites. Typically, they may say: 'I'm not good enough,' or 'I haven't as
much faith as other people.'

The Anglican Diocese of Manchester launched a dioce-
san-wide scheme in 2004 called 'Back to Church Sunday'.
This was then extended nationwide in subsequent years.
Churches that sign up are provided with a well-produced
pack including posters, bookmarks, invitations and welcome booklets to give to newcomers – and also Fairtrade
chocolate to emphasise the role of Christians in promoting

social justice. Congregations use these resources to help them invite neighbours, friends and those on the fringes of church life to come 'back to church'. Holding 'Back to Church Sunday' nationwide on the same day each year means churches benefit from a national publicity campaign.

You don't necessarily have to be part of a national scheme. You could, of course, designate one Sunday a year as a day to invite newcomers or those returning to church after a long absence, and produce your own posters and leaflets.

How to do it:

1. Either join up with the national 'Back to Church Sunday' scheme, or organise your own church's version.
2. Either buy or create the posters, leaflets and other resources that will help congregation members to invite people to one Sunday service.
3. Offer congregation members training in talking naturally about their faith to their friends and handing out invitations; and in welcoming people to church without overwhelming them.
4. Consider the format of your worship for the Sunday in question. How can you make it as accessible as possible to those who may not be used to church or your style of worship?
5. Ensure that your welcome team makes a note of the contact details of new people who appear on that date. If they keep coming to church, keep making them feel welcome. If not, you may want to visit them or ring them after a few weeks.

Further resources:

For more information about 'Back to Church Sunday', see: www.backtochurch.co.uk

99. Go carol-singing around your community.

People can feel more open to the idea of church at Christmas than at other times. Perhaps it's because they associate church with warm memories of carol services and candles. At any rate, many carol services are packed. Unfortunately, before Christmas is also the time when many people are at their most stressed – doing Christmas shopping, preparing food and welcoming relatives. Those living in your community may appreciate it if you bring Christmas to them in the form of carols on the streets, rather than expecting them to come to church.

One Manchester church goes carol-singing around specific streets in its parish each Christmas. As people come to their doors to listen to the carols, a team from the church approach them. The first surprise is that they aren't collecting money for the church, but inviting them to come to Christmas services. The second surprise is that the team offer the residents mince pies. And the third is that they offer to pray for the needs of that family – there and then, if appropriate. The impression is of a church that cares for its community, and the result is that relationships started on those nights have led whole families to start coming to church.

Other churches do something similar, singing carols in shopping centres and giving out mince pies and leaflets – to shoppers and those working in retail outlets. It reinforces the notion that the Church is there to help, and relationships started then can continue through the year. And, if shoppers are interested in coming to your carol services, they can be given leaflets there and then.

How to do it:

1. Organise a team of carol singers from your church. It doesn't have to be the choir or the best singers. Use musicians who can play portable instruments too. You may even want to bring old-fashioned lanterns to complete the image.
2. Recruit a team of people to make or buy large quantities of mince pies. You can organise them into packages, attractively presented, perhaps with some literature about your church and its carol services included.
3. Decide where to focus your efforts, as you can't cover your entire locality: the local estate, the shopping centre or certain specific streets.
4. As your singers work their way through well-known carols, a few 'outriders' can knock on doors to offer people mince pies, or go into shops to offer your packages to the manager or owner. Make sure that they know they should refuse any offer of money.

100. Advertise major events on billboards or bus shelters, or via magazines, local newspapers and local radio.

Occasionally, large churches or groups of churches may put on a large event that requires extra publicity. It might be an ecumenical mission, a holiday club or a series of talks by a high-profile speaker. Obviously, it's important to use all the other methods of communication available to you, such as press releases, posters, leaflets and information in your parish magazine. But it might help to give the event a higher profile to actually pay for adverts in your local news-paper, on billboards or on local radio.

This isn't a cheap option. A tiny newspaper advert, pub-lished once in your local paper is unlikely to have an impact. To create real profile for your event, you may need to pay for a week of adverts, repeated three or four times a day on local radio; or a series of billboards, and adverts on buses, bus shelters and phone boxes. However, if you target such advertising well, people living in your town or city may find themselves unable to escape references to your big event.

There is one project that allows you to make use of national advertising expertise while still keeping references to your local church or set of churches. The Churches Advertising Network (CAN) is a group of Christians work-ing in advertising who create memorable campaigns each Christmas. They pay actors to record broadcast-quality radio adverts that can be played on local commercial sta-tions. And the tagline at the end of the advert links with the tagline on billboards as part of the national advertising cam-paign. It can even be customised to refer to your church or set of churches. All you need to do is raise the necessary funds to help pay for the airtime.

If you end up creating poster or radio adverts yourself, do be aware of some of the principles already discussed in this book: use photos of people, not just text or line drawings, to create effective billboard adverts; use your church's logo, your ecumenical logo, or the special logo you have created for your special event on those posters; and use people 'stories' (i.e. short fictional scripts) to create effective radio adverts, rather than merely information about the event itself.

How to do it:

1. Examine the other methods that you are using to communicate the details about your big event or series of events. Don't pay for airtime or space in your local newspaper if you haven't already sent off press releases, distributed posters and handed out leaflets, as such advertising works best if it reinforces messages that have already been heard elsewhere.

2. Discover the price of radio adverts from your local commercial station, and the price of newspaper adverts from your local newspaper. Don't bother creating adverts unless you can afford to publish or broadcast a decent number of them.

3. If appropriate, contact CAN and customise their Christmas radio adverts to mention your church or group of churches.

4. If you are creating your own newspaper adverts, take advice about the size of the artwork for the newspaper and the format in which it is required. If you have a graphic designer or a poster designer in your congregation, do recruit them to create something appropriate, using photos, logos, colour and exciting typefaces.

5. If you are creating your own radio adverts, take advice

about the quality of recording that you need to provide. You will probably have to write a 20-, 30- or 40-second script, hire a recording studio and record the advert digitally. Or some radio stations will record a script for you for an extra payment.

6. Make sure you get the advert to the newspaper or radio station in time.

7. Monitor its effectiveness, perhaps by asking a selection of those who attend your event where they heard about it. This will help you decide whether such adverts are worth paying for in the future.

Further resources:

For more information about the Churches Advertising Network, see: www.churchads.org.uk